To Pat –
Happy Ch

Mark Gardiner's

**Second Bathroom Book
of
Motorcycle Trivia**

Copyright 2016, Mark Gardiner

Foreword

~~Moron~~ More on the trials, tribulations, and trivialities of motorcycle journalism

I've written half a dozen bike books. Most of them are still available on Amazon, including *Riding Man*, and *On Motorcycles: The Best of Backmarker*. Those two are – in my humble opinion – pretty good reads. *Riding Man* is currently in development as a feature film with a screenplay written by Todd Komarnicki. He wrote the critically acclaimed film *'Sully'*, starring Tom Hanks.

That said, my best-selling book so far has been *Mark Gardiner's Bathroom Book of Motorcycle Trivia*.

A few years ago, I realized that most of my friends had a dog-eared stack of motorcycle magazines on the back of their toilet, that their wives or girlfriends would happily replace with one tidy book containing a year's worth of reading on the john. In 2012, I published that first trivia book, and it sold steadily year over year until 2015, when it hit #1 on Amazon's 'Motorsports' list.

Now, a lot of authors' feelings would be hurt by the realization that their crappiest book outsells their good ones. And my feelings would be hurt too, except for one thing: Nothing balms a bruised ego like a nice royalty check.

In fact, I gave myself one big assignment for 2016, which was to write a sequel – *Mark Gardiner's **Second** Bathroom Book of Motorcycle Trivia.*

The book you're holding is the result. Please don't tell me what you've got in your other hand.

A few words about typos and factual errors...

There almost certainly are a bunch of 'em in here.

In spite of that, I hope that you learn some cool $#!+ every day on the toilet. If I occasionally make you laugh, so much the better. If I occasionally piss you off, well, I suppose that comes with the territory when you embark on a career in journalism.

While I'm on that topic, here is a note about the state of motorcycle journalism...

It's in the toilet. Magazines are cutting staff, few web sites make enough to pay contributors; it's nearly impossible to make a living providing expert content any more. That's why I have taken to monetizing the wealth of motorcycle trivia in my head.

If you like this book, please recommend it to a friend (or better yet, buy another to give as a gift!) If you hate this book, please recommend it to an enemy.

Want to see pictures?

www.BathroomTrivia.com

…contains a searchable archive that will, eventually, include hundreds of images and video links to the subjects covered in both Bathroom Books.

Day 1

The first motorcycle was also the first car
(and vice versa!)

In 1885, Gottlieb Daimler and Wilhelm Maybach built their 'Reitwagen', which most experts agree was the first motorcycle even though it actually had four wheels.

Even the inventors didn't think it was a practical vehicle; it was just a proof-of-concept, rolling on two ungainly wooden wagon wheels, with two outrigger 'training wheels' to keep it upright.

The 1886 "Benz Patent-Motorwagen" is generally considered the first automobile, but it had only three wheels.

Yet another pair of Germans, Hildebrand and Wolfmuller, produced the first commercially-viable motorcycle in 1894. They also coined the term 'motorrad' which means 'motorcycle' in German.

•

As Custer would say,
"Who knew there were so many Indians?"

Indian is the oldest American motorcycle brand that's still in production. But unlike its rival Harley-Davidson (which has been in continuous operation since its founding) the Indian company has been reincarnated so many times you'd think the brand name was a reference to Hindu beliefs about reincarnation, instead of a reference to America's indigenous peoples.

Day 2 – **The founder period: 1901-'16**

George Hendee began making bicycles in 1897. Within a year or two, he produced bicycles under the "American Indian" trademark. Oscar Hedstrom joined the firm in 1900, bringing the engineering know-how needed to produce their first prototype motorcycle.

The first production Indian was the 1902 single. In 1903, Hedstrom set what was then a speed record for motorcycles, at 56 miles an hour. In 1904, the company settled on the fire-engine red color it's now famous for. A year later they built their first v-twin racer.

By 1913, Indian was the most successful of the dozens of motorcycle manufacturers in the U.S. It sold over 30,000 bikes that year. But with success came trouble: The founders had issued so much stock that they no longer had voting control. Oscar Hedstrom proved headstrong, and resigned that year in a dispute with the company's board over what he perceived as stock market manipulation.

In 1916, Hendee announced his retirement, at the age of 50. The company managed to convince Hedstrom to return, which encouraged shareholders. But Hedstrom's second period there was short-lived.

Day 3 – **1930: Indian merges with DuPont**

Hedstrom was ably replaced by Charles B. Franklin, Indian's second great design engineer. Franklin's 'Scout' and 'Chief' models were popular in the Roaring Twenties. Indian also acquired the Ace motorcycle company, and moved production of the Ace inline four-cylinder motor to "the wigwam" in Springfield. All in all, Indians were still very competitive in the marketplace.

But the crash of '29 affected Indian, along with almost every other U.S. company.

Indian's fate was then tied to E. Paul DuPont, a rich industrialist who owned a luxury car company. DuPont arranged to merge his company with Indian in 1930. By 1932, the combined company had abandoned car production (it made less than 600 cars in total) and DuPont had managed to purge Indian's Board of Directors of members he thought were manipulating share prices.

Without DuPont, Indian would have perished in the Depression.

Day 4 – 1945: Under New Ownership (Again)

After WWII, the DuPont family sold its controlling interest to a young industrialist named Ralph B. Rogers.

Rogers acquired both Indian and Torque Manufacturing Co. — a company that had two smaller, vertical-twin models which had been designed by a former Indian employee. Rogers thought those lighter vertical twins would be more popular with returning soldiers who had been exposed to lighter and sportier bikes in Europe.

Decades later, Rogers (who was a dedicated Republican) found himself at odds with Richard Nixon. At the time, Rogers was the chairman of the Public Broadcasting Service. Nixon, who thought PBS was anti-Republican, wanted to cut its funding and force it to drop political commentary. Rogers pushed back and is generally credited with saving PBS.

Day 5 – 1950: Brockhouse is the president, but the brand's headed for the outhouse

John Brockhouse was a third-generation industrialist from England. He was involved in a tantalizing might-have-been project involving a Vincent Rapide-Indian Chief hybrid, but all he really wanted to do was use Indian's U.S. distribution network as a way to sell Norton, AJS, and Royal Enfield motorcycles in the U.S.

In 1953, Indian ceased U.S. production. But Brockhouse Engineering acquired the trademark and sold rebadged Royal Enfield models as Indians until 1960. After that the trademark was briefly owned by Associated Motorcycles (AMC) which made Nortons. AMC sold the name, in turn, to Joseph Berliner.

Day 6 – 1963: Floyd Clymer takes it on

Floyd Clymer (who was perhaps the most irrepressible entrepreneur in American motorcycle history) then attached the Indian name to a variety of frankly ghastly minibikes, mostly acquired from Italjet.

Later in the '60s, Clymer managed to cobble together a (kind'a) cool machine: The Indian 500 Roadster was basically an Italian sport bike — Ceriani fork, Campagnolo twin-leading-shoe front brake, and Borrani rims — powered by a Velocette 500cc single-cylinder motor.

There was some debate about the legality of Clymer's claim to the trademark at all, but he was assigned the trademark by the U.S. Patent and Trademark Office just before he died.

Day 7 – **The 1970s and beyond: Wait, things get even worse...**

Clymer's widow sold the Indian trademark to her husband's ex-lawyer, who continued to import bikes from Italy and Taiwan. The lawyer's company went bankrupt in 1977, and the trademark was claimed by a number of companies — often at the same time — for the next 20 years.

According to USPTO records, the trademark was sold at least eight times between 1970 and 1992. Some guy named Phil Zanghi seems to have sold it to himself a couple of times in that period. Derbi Motor Corp. of America owned it for one day: August 12, 1983.

In 1992, a new entity called American Indian Motorcycle Co. filed a cancellation petition with the USPTO, alleging that any previous trademarks were invalidated by lack of use and because previous claimants had submitted fraudulent information.

In the mid- '90s an entrepreneur/promoter named Wayne Baughman also talked a good game, and even built a couple of prototype 'Century Chiefs' although he does not appear to have ever had a legitimate claim to the famous trademark.

Day 8 – 1997: Indian hits rock bottom

Phil Zanghi never really tried to resurrect Indian. Instead, he used the money he raised from motorcycle-loving investors and licensing deals to fund a luxurious lifestyle including a Rolls Royce and a Ferrari.

In 1997, a U.S. District Court jury deliberated less than three hours before convicting Zanghi of securities fraud, tax evasion, and money laundering. Although he was up for up to 221 years on all charges, he was sentenced to 7 1/2 years.

Zanghi acted as his own lawyer. "Maybe I'm a con man," he told the jury in his closing arguments. "Maybe I'm a promoter. But I brought the Indian trademark back." The trademark was disposed of by a bankruptcy receiver.

[Author's note: I'm not a lawyer, but I have to think that using the phrase "Maybe I'm a con man" was a mistake.]

Day 9 – 1998: Back on the reserve? Maybe not

The next year, Eller Industries announced that it would not only acquire the rights to the trademark from the receiver, but that it would open a factory on a genuine Indian reserve. The company hired famed motorcycle designer James Parker to sketch designs and claimed that Roush Industries developed an engine design.

But it was another case of lots'a smoke, but very little fire. Eller Industries was soon served with a restraining order, when it failed to meet the terms of its contract with the receiver.

That paved the way for a federal bankruptcy judge to allow the sale of the trademark to...

Day 10 – **Indian Motorcycle Company of America**

Gilroy, California was the home of a small manufacturer, the California Motorcycle Company. CMC and several other small companies merged to revive the Indian trademark yet again.

Indian purists thought that selling an Indian with a Harley-clone S&S engine stunk. That was apropos, since Gilroy is the self-proclaimed Garlic Capital of the World.

IMCOA declared bankruptcy in 2003.

Day 11 – **From Gilroy to North Carolina**

Over the years, a few English motorcycles have been sold as Indians. And from 2006-'11, the Indian Motorcycle Company was owned by a London-based private equity firm called Stellican Limited.

Stellican bought the brand and Gilroy assets, and produced a small number of motorcycles out of a new home in Kings Mountain, NC.

Stellican was approximately the 18th company to own the Indian trademark. The company had previously resurrected another iconic American brand, Chris-Craft.

Stellican relaunched Indian in 2009, but sold less than a thousand bikes.

Day 12 – **2011: Polaris seeks a long term victory over Harley-Davidson**

Polaris Industries had a great year in 2010, putting up a record profit at a time when most of the powersports industry was still pretty depressed. But Polaris' Victory motorcycle division still had trouble competing for brand recognition against Harley-Davidson.

That made acquiring Indian a good strategy, and it acquired the trademark from Stellican, which in all honesty was probably glad to get out of the motorcycle business.

Polaris and Indian have, it would seem, a lot to offer each other. The storied Indian brand gives American traditionalists a real alternative to Harley-Davidson, and the brand finally has the kind of financial and engineering backing it has been missing since the 1940s.

Will Polaris provide a long-term home for the Indian brand? Best to (ahem) "reserve" judgment.

•

Day 13 – **Worth Knowing:** *A View to a Kill*

'A View to a Kill' may be one of the worst James Bond films. But while the film was set in the 1980s, with a plot involving horse racing, it was inspired by a short story about *motorcycle riding*.

Ian Fleming created the James Bond character in a series of novels and short stories. *A View to a Kill* was one short story in an anthology titled *'For Your Eyes Only'*.

In the story, Bond investigates the murder of a motorcycle dispatch rider, who was killed while delivering secret documents in France. To catch the killer, Bond impersonates a courier on similar mission. The assassin tries to kill Bond but (of course) the spy is ready for him. Bond kills the killer, and then uncovers his hidden base of operations.

Cool fact: Spy novelist Ian Fleming worked in the British Naval Intelligence Division during WWII. He was involved in the creation and oversight of 30 Assault Unit – an elite commando group. The plot of *A View to a Kill* is fairly similar to some of the things that the commandos of 30 Assault Unit actually did.

•

Day 14 – **Weirdly compelling motorcycle movie:** ***Roadside Prophets***

This 1992 film was written and directed by Abbe Wool (she also wrote the critically acclaimed *Sid and Nancy* screenplay.)

'Prophets…' is a wacky road-movie that stars L.A. punk icon John Doe and the Beastie Boys' Adam Horovitz. They're two guys on Harleys, riding from L.A. to Nevada, looking for a place to dispose of a comrade's ashes.

Wool roped in an incredible cast of supporting actors, from John Cusack to Timothy Leary (the LSD guru) and Arlo Guthrie. The script is antic, but the cast makes it all work. Doe also scored the film, and the music's great.

Day 15 – **A web site worth knowing: Silodrome**

www.silodrome.com calls itself "gasoline culture" and as such, it covers cars and boats too. But, it skews motorcycle, with near-daily updates on topics ranging from new-but-obscure bikes to customs, to rediscovered bikes, films, and photos.

The site's characterized by better than average photos and much better than average writing. One fun recurring theme is "The Top Five Vintage Motorcycles on eBay This Week". You can save yourself hours of eBay trolling by just checking in with Silodrome.

•

Day 16 – **Valentino "The Doctor" Rossi**

Valentino Rossi is the only active racer who can lay a legitimate claim to being the GOAT — greatest of all time. He's won World Championship road races in three different decades, in four different classes, and for four different manufacturers. I could easily fill an entire book with Rossi trivia (and such is his popularity, it would sell well!) But… I won't.

Rossi's career at the top level spans the 500GP and MotoGP eras. He's won the top championship seven times (so far!) He's the only motorcycle racer that many non-fans can identify. He's also the only contemporary rider with any chance of reaching Giacomo Agostini's career total of 122 race wins in the World Championship.

I just threw a lot of numbers at you, but here's eleven more Rossi facts that even some fairly devoted fans may not know.

Day 17 – **Like father, like son**

Rossi's dad, Graziano, raced in the World Championship between 1977 and '82.

Graziano's best season was 1979. Riding a Morbidelli in the 250cc class, he won three races and finished third in the championship. His best result in the 500cc class was a second place, at the Dutch TT in 1980.

Rossi's mom, Stefania, thought motorcycle racing was too dangerous for her son, and she argued that, instead, he should race go-karts. He won a regional karting championship in 1990, when he was ten. After that, he switched to minimotos.

Day 18 – **What's the opposite of 'sophomore jinx'?**

Rossi entered the World Championships in 1996, in the 125cc class. He experienced the opposite of the 'sophomore jinx', because he won the 125cc title in his second year in that class.

He moved up to the 250cc class in 1998 and won *that* championship in his second year.

Then, he moved up to the 500cc class in 2000 and won *that one* in his second year, too!

In 2002, the top class in the World Championship switched technical rules. 500cc two-strokes were replaced with 990cc four-strokes. That was the beginning of the

MotoGP era. Rossi didn't wait for his second season in MotoGP to win that class. In fact, he didn't even wait for the end of the season; he won the inaugural MotoGP World Championship with four races to go.

Day 19 – **Honda, Schmonda**

For the 2004 season, Rossi jumped from Honda to Yamaha, for a reported salary of $12 million—making him by far the highest-paid motorcycle racer of all time. The first race of the '04 season took place in South Africa; Rossi won it, and became the first motorcycle racer in history to win consecutive World Championship races for two different manufacturers.

Day 20 – **Head games**

Although he should be famous only for his talent on the track, Rossi's also famous for his off-track rivalries. After a multi-year battle of egos with fellow Italian Max Biaggi, Rossi's foremost rival during that 2004 season was a Spaniard, Sete Gibernau.

The 13th race of the 2004 season took place at Qatar. After qualifying, Rossi's team was caught cleaning the Champ's grid position. That was a violation of the rules, and Rossi was penalized; he had to start the race from the back of the grid.

Rossi believed that it was Sete Gibernau's team (Honda) that ratted him out to the race officials. Gibernau went on to win that race, and in a fit of pique, Rossi told reporters that Gibernau would never win another race. Whether that was a premonition or a curse, it was true; Sete never did win another race, and retired a couple of years later.

Day 21 – **Dark days at Ducati**

In 2011, Rossi switched manufacturers again when he signed a two-year deal to race for Ducati, with American Nicky Hayden as his team-mate.

Although Casey Stoner had been successful on the Ducati 'Desmosedici' machine, neither Rossi nor Hayden ever really came to terms with it. In his two seasons at Ducati, Rossi stood on the podium only three times; he never won a race. He finished 7th overall in 2011 and could do no better than 6th overall in 2012.

Day 22 – **Machiavelli was Italian, too**

After two years in purgatory, Rossi returned to the Yamaha factory team. He shocked quite a few die-hard fans when he fired his long-time crew chief Jeremy Burgess, and replaced him with Silvano Galbusera, who had previously worked for the Yamaha World Superbike team. Rossi met Galbusera in 2010, when he briefly rode a Yamaha superbike to test his fitness, as he recovered from a broken leg.

Although Burgess' feelings were hurt and he expressed doubt that Rossi would do any better with Galbusera, the champ immediately returned to form.

Day 23 – **Fame is taxing, eh?**

In 2007, Italian tax officials investigated Rossi for tax evasion. The basis of the tax case was that Rossi claimed most of his business interests were based in Britain, although he continued to live in Italy. This arrangement allowed him to pay UK taxes, which were far lower than those in Italy. In years when he made tens of millions of dollars, Rossi declared only 500 Euros on his Italian income tax.

In February, 2008 Rossi reached a 35 million Euro settlement with the Italian government.

Day 24 – **People will talk...**

For years, Rossi was accompanied by a male friend—Alessio 'Uccio' Salucci—almost everywhere he went. This unsurprisingly led to rumors that he was gay. For what it's worth, Rossi races with the letters 'WLF' on his leathers. He says that the W is really two Vs, and that it's an acronym for 'ViVa La Figa'. That's Italian for 'long live pussy'.

Day 25 – **When is #1 not #1? When it's 46**

As a multi-time World Champion, Rossi has often earned the right to carry the #1 number plate. But, he has always raced with the number 46. That was Graziano Rossi's competitor number when he scored his World Championship victories in 1979.

His determination to ride with number 46 — even in seasons when the FIM would prefer he carried the #1 plate — could be seen as honoring his dad, Graziano. But it's probably more about selling t-shirts with his trademarked '46'.

Day 26 – **Ay, Chihuahua!**

Rossi has another cryptic slogan on his crash helmet, which reads 'Tribu dei Chihuahua'. This goes back to his days as a schoolboy in Tavullia, Italy. He and his friends called themselves 'The Chihuahua Gang' (loosely translated).

Day 27 – **Pizza with GOAT cheese**

Rossi's hometown is Tavullia, which is just east of San Marino and near the famed Misano race track. His fan club is headquartered in the Ristorante Pizzeria Da Rossi. It's a Mecca for Rossi fans whenever he's racing—if you can get anywhere near it, for the crowds. They watch the races on the restaurant's giant TVs. Even if you're not a Rossi fan, the pizza's pretty good!

•

Day 28 – **Weirdly compelling motorcycle movie:** *Mammuth*

Gérard Depardieu stars in this French road movie, which was presumably *not* named after the Munch Mammuth motorcycle he rides.

Rather, Depardieu represents a disenfranchised and frustrated worker seeking the retirement benefits owed to him. He's an obsolete blue-collar worker, a type about to become extinct – like the wooly mammoth.

This movie's been described as a cross between *Amelie* and *The Wrestler*.

Day 29 – **A web site worth knowing: MotoMatters**

www.motomatters.com is the site for people who want to take a deep dive into MotoGP (and to a lesser extent World Superbikes.)

This blog is a labor of love mostly written by one man, David Emmett. He's an English ex-pat living in Holland, who's attended virtually every MotoGP race over the last decade. In that time, he's developed a lot of connections with insiders. So, Emmett's not just a good source of racing news, his web site is a good place to go, if you're trying to sort truth from rumors.

•

Motorcycles in space! (OK, in the space *program*.)

In 1969, NASA celebrated the first man on the moon. But the administration was also planning future missions, and knew that sending future astronauts to the moon with some kind of lunar vehicle would have both scientific value and propaganda value; it was another way to one-up their Soviet rivals. Boeing and General Motors got a contract to develop the Lunar Roving Vehicle.

But did you know that NASA also experimented with the idea of lunar motorcycles?

Day 30 – – Astronaut bikers

Neil Armstrong, the first man to set foot on the moon, rode dirt bikes. While he was on the moon, Montesa boss Pedro Permanyer arranged to have a motorcycle dropped off at his home. Armstrong only kept it after Permanyer assured him that Montesa did not expect any publicity in return. The third man on the moon, Pete Conrad, was also an avid motorcyclist. He died of a heart attack, hours after crashing his Harley-Davidson near Ojai, California.

Day 31 – **You meet the nicest people on ~~a Honda~~ the moon**

The moon motorcycle was a project of the Manned Spacecraft Center in Houston. Engineers there began their research by buying a stock Honda CT90 trail bike. They tested that bike, to see if an astronaut in a space suit could control it on various sandy and gravel surfaces. They also test-rode it in an elaborate rig that used pulleys and counterweights to simulate riding in the moon's reduced gravity.

Eventually, NASA engineers realized that in the moon's $1/6^{th}$ g, a motorcycle would have to lean much further to turn. At that point, they decided to try a fat-tired lunar minibike, with the proportions of a Honda Z50 'monkey bike'. They even tested that concept in the famous 'Vomit Comet'—a cargo plane that flew a parabolic climb/dive pattern to simulate reduced gravity.

Day 32 – **Motorcycles on the moon? Shocking.**

NASA then developed a working electric minibike, with similar proportions to a Z50, but with a somewhat taller handlebar and longer wheelbase, because they'd determined that astronauts' suits made it hard to crouch on the tiny cycle.

The prototype had a ten-pound, $5/8^{th}$ horsepower motor and a 30 amp-hour battery. It had a top speed of seven miles an hour. The minibike was functional, and was considered for the Apollo 15 mission, in spite of the fact that the cycle had trouble towing the Modular Equipment Transporter (a lightweight utility trailer that astronauts called 'the rickshaw'.)

The moon motorbike was killed off once and for all when Boeing and GM developed the Rover ahead of schedule. The Rover was ready in time for Apollo 15 in the summer of 1971, so the moon motorcycle never got its chance.

•

Day 33 – **A web site worth knowing: Common Tread**

http://www.revzilla.com/common-tread is the only website on my 'worth knowing' list that serves an overtly commercial purpose. While most of the other sites I've singled out in this book are commercial in the sense that they're a job for someone, most of them at least began as labors of love. Not Common Tread. It exists only to drive traffic to the Revzilla online moto-retailer. That said, the daily-updated site is expertly edited by Lance Oliver, an experienced motorcycle journalist who has a knack for finding writers and presenting stories that resonate with ordinary motorcyclists.

Too many other sites present motorcycle journalism that, between the lines, tells readers they'll never be as fast or get invited to as many cool parties, and they'll certainly never ride as many cool bikes. Common Tread has, admirably, retained a common touch.

•

Harley-Davidson's dead ends

As the oldest motorcycle company in continuous operation, Harley-Davidson's obviously seen its share of successes. And, the company's product line makes a fetish of tradition, so it's not exactly under pressure to try a lot of new things.

Still, every now and then Harley-Davidson does think outside of the denim-and-leather-covered box. Customers, or management (or sometimes both) usually end up hating those things. Historically, when Harley strays from the air-cooled, pushrod v-twin cruiser format, it's punished.

Here's a look at a few dead ends, including some bikes that customers rejected and that are now sought-after.

Day 34 – **Nova? Or 'no va'?**

In the late 1970s, Harley spent millions on the Nova project; designing and prototyping v-twin, v-four, and v-six motorcycles ranging from 800-1,500cc displacement. The Nova motors would be liquid-cooled, with overhead cams. The intent was to take on increasingly sophisticated and powerful bikes coming from Japan.

So, what killed the Nova? It wasn't a technical problem; it was corporate bureaucracy.

At the time, Harley-Davidson was owned by American Machine and Foundry. AMF had two divisions, one focused on industrial equipment and the other focused on leisure products.

A change in AMF management led to a new strategy. They decided to use the leisure division as a cash cow (or should I say, 'cash hog'?) while pumping capital investment into the industrial division. Harley had already spent about $15 million on the Nova project, with 30 working prototype motors and a dozen complete bikes, but there was no way

AMF would allow the company to make the capital investment required for new tooling and assembly lines.

Ironically, the decision to kill the Nova project helped create the circumstances that led Vaughn Beals' employee buyout, and ultimately saved Harley-Davidson from a slow death under AMF control.

Day 35 – **They were into VR before 'VR' meant VR**

The Harley-Davidson VR 1000 had a frustrating history in AMA Superbike racing. The idea of building a competitive superbike first occurred to a small, renegade group in Milwaukee, in 1988.

It may have been a case of too many cooks spoiling the broth. Harley farmed out most of the v-twin motor's design to Roush Racing. Steve Scheibe, an engineer at Roush ended up moving to Harley to manage the project. Scheibe brought in a friend, Pete Mohar, who ran an engineering consultancy called Gemini Technology Systems to work on other aspects of the bike, while the chassis was the responsibility of Mike Eatough.

They were all smart guys but the VR 1000 took a long time to get off the drawing board. It was conceived in 1988, but wasn't raced until '96. In that interval, competitors' bikes improved by leaps and bounds. Harley hired Miguel Duhamel, who'd spent the previous season racing in the 500GP World Championship, but even he wasn't really competitive on it.

Harley stuck with the VR 1000 for five racing seasons. The bike showed flashes of brilliance, such as the time Chris Carr put it on the pole for a Superbike race in

Pomona, or the time Tom Wilson crossed the finish line first at Mid-Ohio, only to have the results put back a lap due to a red flag. They killed the project in 2001.

Day 36 – **How do you say 'Harley' in Italian?**

Considering that underwhelming Superbike history, you may be surprised to learn that Harley-Davidson actually won several Grand Prix World Championships in the mid-1970s. Americans hardly knew it was even happening; it was an all-Italian effort.

Aermacchi was an Italian company that started out in the airplane business, but shifted into motorcycles after WWII. In 1960, Harley-Davidson acquired a 50% interest in the Italian company, because Harley dealers needed smaller entry-level bikes for customers who weren't ready (or couldn't afford) a big v-twin. Aermacchi designed and built the 250cc 'Sprint' for U.S. sales. Meanwhile, its racing team developed some fast two-stroke twins, like Yamaha's Grand Prix racers.

In 1974, AMF acquired the rest of the shares in Aermacchi. Those Grand Prix racers were rebadged as Harley-Davidsons, and Walter Villa won The Motor Company its only World Championships from 1974-'76.

Although Aermacchi was obviously capable of hand-building a few top quality race bikes, the company's mass-production fell further and further behind Japanese imports in terms of both performance and build quality. AMF sold Aermacchi to the Cagiva Group in 1978.

Day 37 – **Was it a Blast? Not really**

Decades later, Harley-Davidson tried to produce an entry-level bike again with the ill-fated Buell Blast, sold (read: almost given away) from 2000 to 2010.

The Blast was a small, light motorcycle with a relatively (for Harley) sporting stance. Basically, the motor was a 1,000cc Sportster missing the rear cylinder. The bodywork was made out of Surlyn plastic—a material normally used in golf balls. Presumably that was to make it crash resistant.

It was a good idea. Really, it was. And according to Harley's PR, the Blast was used to train over 175,000 riders in the Rider's Edge program. But it was so unloved that Buell crushed the Blasts into cubes.

Day 38 – **Why 'Servi-Car'?**
　　　　　Because it was for servicing cars

Considering that it was offered in the Harley-Davidson lineup from 1932 to '74, it's hard to call the three-wheeled Servi-Car a dead end. But few Servi-Cars ever served their initial purpose.

Back in the 1930s, quite a few garages offered to pick up and drop off customers' cars. (Imagine that, eh? Customer service!)

The idea was, garage operators would send a man out on the Harley to collect the customer's car. The delivery driver would then attach the trike to the customer's car's bumper, and tow it back to the garage. After servicing the customer's car, they'd return it to the customer with the

Harley in tow. Then they'd unhitch the hog and return to the garage.

The initial concept didn't catch on all that well, but the idea of a small, fuel-efficient vehicle with a large cargo capacity found a niche with police departments and all manner of delivery services and tradesmen.

Day 39 – **Americans drink coffee, not 'café'**

By the mid-1970s, the glory days of the British café-racer scene were past. But that didn't prevent Harley from finally taking a stab at a café racer of its own. Willie G. Davidson created the XLCR by grafting the front of a Sportster onto the rear subframe and swingarm of an XR750.

It looked the business, as they'd say in Britain, thanks to the bikini fairing and blacked-out motor and exhausts. And it did have some significant upgrades, including far better brakes and Morris alloy wheels. It was buzz-worthy, at its launch in 1977. But the experts of the day concluded it was still too heavy, and scary fast only in the sense that the stock frame imparted a threatening weave at anything over 90 miles an hour.

It was a new model for only three years, although some dealers had XLCRs languish on their sales floors well into the '80s. Ironically (and predictably) it's now one of the more desirable late- '70s hogs.

Day 40 – **XR1200x**

Harley's execs must've forgotten the lessons of the XLCR, because they released the sport-oriented XR1200x

Sportster in Europe in 2010. The U.S. market got the bike a year later.

Journalists (I was one of them) were pleasantly surprised by the bike's handling. In spite of weighing nearly 600 pounds, the Showa fork and shock, and 4-piston Nissin front brakes made it by far the best-handling Harley in recent memory. With its wide handlebar, 18" front wheel, and mid-mounted controls it wasn't exactly a sport bike, but it was capable of hanging with most imports on a twisting road.

Harley put a sport-oriented marketing push behind it, too; sponsoring a spec-racing class at AMA Pro Racing road races. In spite of that—or perhaps because of that—Harley's customers never knew what to make of it. Just two years after its U.S. introduction, the model was allowed to die on the vine.

•

Day 41 – **Weirdly compelling motorcycle movie:** *Akira*

This Japanese animated feature didn't get much love outside Japan when it was released in 1988. But over time, it's been recognized as an anime masterpiece.

The film's set in 2019, in a Tokyo that's been ravaged by WWIII. Scientists perform an experiment on a member of a motorcycle gang, giving him psychic powers. The plot's not that easy to follow, but the animation is still fabulous – perhaps even more so now that it's technically out-of-date.

I'm not recommending illegal drug use, but I bet it's even better if you're high. Katshuiro Otomo was a big influence on the Wachowski Brothers (now, I suppose, I should call them sisters) and without *Akira*, there would never have been *The Matrix*.

·

Day 42 – **What was the all-time best motorcycle movie? That's Easy (Rider)**

After a bunch of 1960s "bikesploitation" movies, Easy Rider (released in 1969) was still capable of shocking the critics. Mainly, because it was not bad.

The film was written by Dennis Hopper, Peter Fonda, and Terry Southern. The latter was a beatnik with a knack for finding himself wherever the best booze and dope, and prettiest girls with the most questionable virtues congregated.

Hopper and Fonda star as two drug runners who, after a big payoff, head from L.A. to New Orleans on a road trip. Two hippies traveling through the conservative American south; what could go wrong, eh? The first time they're locked up, they're luckily thrown into the hoosegow with a drunken ACLU lawyer.

The lawyer was played by Jack Nicholson in a role that earned him an Oscar nomination. Nicholson's character gets them out and accompanies them on their journey.

The road trip ends badly, but Hopper was celebrated at the Cannes Film Festival. (See previous note about booze, dope, and girls.)

That much is generally agreed, although many aspects of Easy Rider's creation are now debated, even by the people who were involved in the film. There's an old expression: "If you remember the '60s, you weren't really there." That's perhaps also true of Easy Rider.

Day 43 – **Choosing a few bikes**

The bikes seen in the film were Harley-Davidson panheads that had previously been used by the LAPD. Tex Hall (a stuntman) and Dan 'Grizzly Adams' Haggerty were in charge of coordinating the four motorcycles used on the shoot. The choppers were built over the course of a month by two African-American bikers, Cliff Vaughs and Ben Hardy. They were members of the 'Chosen Few', which was a racially integrated bike gang.

Vaughs had a day job, working in the news room at KRLA, a radio station. He met Fonda in 1966, when he covered the actor's trial for possession of marijuana. They struck up a conversation about motorcycles. Soon afterward, Fonda and Dennis Hopper came by Vaughs' apartment to discuss their idea for a motorcycle movie.

It's possible that one of the reasons people have such disparate recollections of what exactly happened during the film's production is that one thing most agree on is this: You know the scenes where they're smoking pot? It was definitely real pot.

Day 44 – **On the road again**

You've probably gone on motorcycle road trips that were better-planned and more organized than the Easy Rider shoot.

The basic premise of the movie occurred to Peter Fonda after he was inspired by a production still of himself and Bruce Dern on the set of 'Wild Angels'. On the spur of the moment, he decided he wanted to make "a modern western where two guys travel around the country and eventually get shot by hillbillies." That's deep, eh? He wanted to call it, 'The Loners'. Fonda and Hopper brought in Terry Southern as screenwriter, and he came up with the title Easy Rider.

The film shoot was an actual road trip, and it was done for $360,000—peanuts even in 1969. The crew moved in a motor home with one five-ton truck carrying gear. The stars often rode the motorcycles from point to point (although I've read that they loaded the motorcycles into the truck to cross Texas, because they were afraid they might actually live out the script too closely!)

The good folks at Eagle Rider have mapped out a route that follows the film crew on their road trip from L.A. to New Orleans. Google it.

Day 45 – **The sole surviving movie bike (both of them)**

At least two of the four choppers (there were two 'Captain America' bikes, and two of the ones Hopper rode) were damaged in filming. And, as the story goes, at least three of the four were stolen after the shoot.

In 1996, however, Dan Haggerty claimed to have restored the one surviving 'Captain America' chopper. He sold it to a collector and it now resides in the (self-proclaimed) National Motorcycle Museum in Anamosa, Iowa.

That would seem credible, except that Haggerty did it again, claiming *another* Captain America chopper was the sole surviving bike. That one sold for over a million bucks at auction in 2014. Haggerty himself died in 2016, so I suppose the secret—if he knew it—died with him.

Day 46 – **As motorcyclists, they were star-crossed**

Peter Fonda was a die-hard motorcyclist before Easy Rider, and has remained one. He's owned everything from dirt bikes to cruisers to an MV Agusta F4. His first painful lesson in the consequences of riding without proper gear came in 1964, when he crashed a Triumph on Mullholland Drive in Los Angeles, while wearing nothing but a bathing suit and loafers.

In 1985, he broke his neck and back in a crash that left him half-an-inch shorter! And in 1993 he hit a deer, crashing heavily again. Still, Fonda's luck was better than Dan Haggerty's. Haggerty once crashed and broke his left leg. That wasn't so bad, but a post-operative infection nearly cost him his leg. He once claimed that the Pope wrote him a 'get well' letter.

I don't know whether the Pope was a fan of 'The Life and Times of Grizzly Adams' or Haggerty's portrayal of a biker in 'Bury Me an Angel'.

•

The Grand Slam of American motorcycle racing

From 1954 through 1985, the AMA Grand National Championship was awarded to the rider who accumulated the most points in as many as 35 races, held on road courses, mile and half-mile ovals, and TT courses (held on dirt, with at least one right turn and a jump). Short track races were added into the mix in 1961.

Only a handful of riders have ever managed to win a 'National' on every type of track. Getting at least one career win on all five types of track is known as a 'Grand Slam'. It calls for not just talent, but versatility.

Here are profiles of the riders who've won the Grand Slam...

Day 47 – **Slam minus 1, but no less impressive for it**

Joe Leonard achieved it first, and fastest.

- Mile: San Mateo, CA July 19, 1953
- Road race: Windber, PA July 26, 1953
- Half-mile: Sturgis, SD August 6, 1953
- TT: Peoria, IL August 30, 1953

All in the span of one month and 11 days!

Leonard's considered the first Grand Slam winner, even though he achieved it before short track races were part of the Grand National Championship. He was more than just a versatile motorcycle racer; after a storied career on two wheels, he came close to winning the Indy 500 in 1968. He won the USAC championship twice in the 1970s.

Racing was probably safer than his first job in motorcycling. When he was still a teenager in San Diego, he worked at a motorcycle shop near a naval base. Sailors often came in to buy motorcycles without knowing how to ride them. When that happened, the owner of the shop sent

Joe out, to ride on the back of sailors' bikes while shouting instructions about how to clutch, brake, etc.

Day 48 – **Call him 'Bugsy'**

The next man to score an AMA Grand Slam was Dick 'Bugsy' Mann.

- TT: Peoria, IL August 30, 1959
- Road race: Laconia, NH June 19, 1960
- Half-mile: Heidelberg, PA June 11, 1961
- Short track: Hinsdale, IL August 15, 1969
- Mile: Homewood, IL August 5, 1972

All told, Mann took nearly 13 years to compile his Grand Slam, but he didn't celebrate extra-hard after that victory in Homewood—mainly because the idea of the Grand Slam hadn't yet occurred to anyone. It only entered the American motorcycle racing lexicon *after* Mann achieved the feat.

He was, if anything, even more versatile than his Grand National Championship record suggests. He was also a serious motocross competitor. And after he retired from the GNC, he raced in the International Six Days Trial on the Isle of Man in 1975, earning a bronze medal.

Dick's nickname predates his motorcycle racing career. His older brother got the nickname 'Bugs' and beginning around the fourth grade, his friends started calling him 'Little Bugs'.

Day 49 – **The King**

Kenny Roberts

- Short track: Houston Astrodome, January 29, 1972

- Mile: Colorado Springs, CA July 7, 1973
- Half-mile: Gardena, CA October 6 1973
- Road race: Road Atlanta, GA June 2, 1974
- TT: Peoria, IL August 18, 1974

Roberts eventually left the Grand National Championship because his sponsor, Yamaha, couldn't deliver a competitive flat track bike. That was a blessing in disguise, because he left the GNC for Grands Prix, becoming the first American to win the 500GP World Championship.

Day 50 – **A career cut short**

Bubba Shobert

- Mile: Indianapolis, IN July 3, 1982
- Short track: San Jose, CA May 5, 1984
- Road race: Mid-Ohio, September 30, 1984
- TT: Gardena, CA March 30, 1985
- Half-mile: Phoenix, AZ April 26, 1986

Like Roberts, Bubba Shobert left the Grand National Championship for the World Championship. His promising Grand Prix career was cut short by a horrific accident on the 'cool-down' lap after the 1989 Laguna Seca GP. Shobert rode into the back of Kevin McGee, who had stopped in the middle of the track to do a burnout for the fans.

Smoking is bad for you, don'cha know.

Day 51 – **DC10 lands on the list**

The last man to record a Grand Slam was Doug Chandler.

- Short track: Hinsdale, IL July 22, 1983
- TT: Gardena, CA April 7, 1984

- Mile: San Jose, CA Sept 14, 1986
- Half-mile: Gardena, CA September 20, 1986
- Road race: Mid-Ohio, August 20, 1989

By the time Chandler scored his road race win, the AMA had split the road racing and dirt track championships. Chandler's credited with his Grand Slam by virtue of winning an AMA Superbike race at Mid-Ohio in 1989. (By then, the AMA had made Superbikes the official 'national championship' class.)

Day 52 – Will anyone else ever join this elite club?

The best candidate is probably Nicky Hayden. He's an extremely accomplished dirt track racer, who's already won AMA Nationals on short track, TT, and half-mile ovals. He's won a bunch of AMA Superbike races, leaving only a mile track left to win.

Hayden left the AMA Superbike Championship for Grands Prix in 2003, and moved to the World Superbike Championship in 2016.

He's no longer a spring chicken, but seven different GNC riders have won flat track races while in their forties. I would not rule out Nicky's return to his dirt track roots at some point in the future. I know he thinks about the possibility of winning a race on a mile oval, because I've discussed it with him.

•

Day 53 – Worth Knowing: The Wright Brothers

The Wright Brothers were bicycle builders before they built the world's first successful airplane. In fact, one of the reasons they succeeded where other pioneer aviators had failed (often fatally) was that they correctly guessed that an airplane should lean into a turn like a bicycle.

In the late 1890s, there were quite a few people trying to make the first flying machine, and several rivals were as capable as the Wright Brothers when it came to generating power and lift. The Wrights succeeded because they were the first people with a plane they could control.

Wilbur Wright was also the first person to accurately describe countersteering – which is perhaps the single most important riding skill, when it comes to your safety. This is what he said about it:

> *I have asked dozens of bicycle riders how they turn to the left. I have never found a single person who stated all the facts correctly when first asked. They almost invariably said that to turn to the left, they turned the handlebar to the left and as a result made a turn to the left. But on further questioning them, some would agree that they first turned the handlebar a little to the right, and then as the machine inclined to the left, they turned the handlebar to the left and as a result made the circle, inclining inward.*

•

Stunts gone bad

"It's only funny until someone puts an eye out," they warn. Then, it's fucking hilarious.

You have to admit that it's more entertaining when things go seriously pear-shaped. With that in mind, here are a few stories about stunts that went very wrong...

Day 54 – **Inspiring generations of little boys to visit their local ER**

Robert Craig Knievel was an avid motorcycle rider and semi-pro hockey player who grew up in hardscrabble Montana mining country. His moral compass was imprecise—to say the least—but he was a natural when it came to promotion. In 1960, Knievel arranged for his hockey team to play a demonstration game against the Czech national team (in the U.S. for the Olympics.) Knievel left the arena early after being ejected from the game, and the gate receipts were never found.

Growing up, he was known as Bobby, and there are at least two different stories about how he got his 'Evel' nickname.

According to one story, Knievel spent a night in the Butte, MO jail in a cell beside a local recidivist named Arthur Knofel. The Butte cops knew that guy as 'Awful Knofel' and some jailer assigned young Bobby the nickname of 'Evil Knievel'.

Another story attributes the nickname to Bob Blair, one of his early motorcycle sponsors. Blair thought the name 'Bobby Knievel and his Motorcycle Daredevils' was lame, and suggested 'Evil Knievel' instead.

Bobby thought calling himself 'Evil' would remind people of the Hells Angels, so he compromised and went with 'Evel'.

Day 55 – "Pictures or it didn't happen"

Evel jumped the fountains at Caesar's Palace casino in Las Vegas on Dec. 31, 1967.

In the weeks leading up to the jump, he attempted to convince the ABC television network to buy the TV rights. ABC demurred, but told him that if he shot it himself, they'd consider buying the film after the fact. Knievel then convinced his friend John Derek to film it.

Evel came up short, and the ensuing crash broke his pelvis, hip, femur, and both ankles, among other things. He suffered a concussion and—so the story goes—was in a coma for month. Needless to say, the film was worth a lot more because he'd crashed.

Interesting note: John Derek was married to actress Linda Evans at the time, and she operated one of the cameras that day. Later on, he was married to actress Bo Derek, of '10' fame. He photographed both of them, at different times, for nude spreads in Playboy.

Day 56 – 'Bus'ted, again

Eight years later, ABC's Wide World of Sports was eager to cover Knievel's attempt to jump 13 buses in London's Wembley Stadium.

90,000 thousand fans watched him crash again. In spite of a fractured pelvis, Evel got to his feet and addressed the crowd.

"Ladies and gentlemen of this wonderful country," Evel said, "I've got to tell you that you are the last people in the world who will ever see me jump. Because I will never, ever, ever jump again. I'm through."

Day 57 – Biker Build-off get-off

'Indian Larry' Desmedt was a Brooklyn-based chopper builder who was known for riding his creations while standing on the seat. He died in 2004, after crashing while performing that stunt in front of a large crowd in a Charlotte, NC parking lot.

He was in Charlotte for the filming of an episode of Discovery Channel's 'Biker Build-Off' reality show. Too bad they weren't filming 'Biker Get-Off'—he would'a won that for sure, and scored extra points for choosing to do his stunt without a helmet.

Indian Larry apprenticed with Ed 'Big Daddy' Roth. After his return to New York, Larry was a frequent subject of the art-world photographer Robert Mapplethorpe, who was drawn to the biker's fast-and-loose lifestyle.

Larry thought of himself as an artist, too. He was survived by his wife, a burlesque performer known as 'Bambi the Mermaid of Coney Island'.

Day 58 – A guy who needed a second opinion from an odds-maker

Perhaps one of the most horrific stunts-gone-wrong was Clint Ewing's failed attempt to set a Guinness-approved record for the longest motorcycle ride through a fire tunnel.

Ewing's stunt was performed in Sturgis in 2013, in front of a huge crowd and (of course) TV cameras. The plan was for him to ride a 360-foot tunnel made of chicken wire and gasoline-soaked cardboard. All things considered, I suppose that when the 32 year-old Californian escaped with third-degree burns over 12% of his body, he got off light.

The crazy thing was, Country Music Television interviewed him from his hospital bed. He told CMT that when he was planning the stunt he estimated that he had an 85% chance of succeeding.

Day 59 – **Cops put on an arresting display**

Plant City, FL is a town of 25,000 people about 25 miles east of Tampa. The local police department used to have about 100 employees, of whom 74 were sworn peace officers. I'm not sure if Plant City was a haven for criminals or what, but that's about twice the number of cops, per capita, among comparable American cities.

In 2002, a federal prosecutor alleged that the local police chief had conspired to hide evidence in a corruption investigation. A few years later, the chief invited the local Chamber of Commerce to tour the station

and have lunch; maybe he thought it would be a good public relations move.

Part of the demonstration involved seating the department's guests in a small bleacher set up in the parking lot, so they could see Plant City's motorcycle cops demonstrate their riding skills.

As one of those guests noted, she just had time to think, "I hope his brakes work," as a cop headed straight into the bleachers at high speed. Two women were treated for broken legs and ankles.

Day 60 – **Roland Sands rolls offstage**

Custom-bike star Roland Sands was born to be in the motorcycle industry – his parents owned Performance Machine. In the '90s he was a star in the hard-fought AMA 250GP class. Then, he started his own RSD custom parts business.

But he may unfortunately be best known for that one time he rode the new Indian FTR flat track racing motorcycle onto the Buffalo Chip stage in Sturgis. As an ex-road racer, he's probably a 'front brake' kind'a guy, but flat track race bikes don't have front brakes.

Maybe that was why he rode the bike onto the stage and rolled right across the stage, off the other side, and into the crowd. Four spectators were injured. Roland's own injuries were mostly limited to a bruised ego.

•

Day 61 – **A web site worth knowing: MotorcycleRoads.com**

www.motorcycleroads.com is the creation of a guy named Bill Belei. He was an avid motorcyclist who served in the U.S. military for 25 years, during which time he was stationed at over a dozen bases.

That lifestyle gave him the chance to ride great roads all across the U.S. Beginning in 2011, Bill began compiling a searchable database of thousands of great roads. No matter where you live, you can get great advice, including downloadable maps and GPX files for a ride, even information on where to stay or eat and how often you'll come across gas stations.

Not fancy, but deep and well-organized. A terrific resource for sport bike rider, sport-tourers, and tourers – especially if you're riding in a new area.

•

Day 62 – Weirdly compelling motorcycle movie: *Under the Skin*

This recent film was made by Jonathan Glazer, who is not particularly well-known in the feature film world, but is a star in the advertising genre.

The movie's based on a science fiction novel in which an alien, disguised as a beautiful woman, travels around the Scottish Highlands killing and eating people. There's no gore in Glazer's version, but if some of the acting seems strikingly naturalistic, it's because many of the interactions between Scarlett Johansson and supporting actors were filmed with real people, using hidden cameras. They were only approached by the crew after the fact, and asked if their scenes could be incorporated into the film.

Johansson is shadowed by a man on a motorcycle, who is played by a real-life motorcycle racing star: Jeremy McWilliams.

•

Day 63 – **How motocross jumped in popularity**

It's hard to believe that the U.S.—now the sole MX superpower—used to be a third-world country when it came to motocross. In the early days of MX, countries like Belgium and Sweden kicked our ass.

The credit for introducing the U.S. to the sport of motocross goes to one guy: Edison Dye. He was a flamboyant promoter with an eye for flashy cars, foppish clothes, and fast women. He was also the U.S. importer for Husqvarna motorcycles in the '60s, and brought top European racers to the U.S. after the World Championship season had ended. By doing so, he gave the first generation of American racers something to shoot for.

Day 64 – **Motocross, you say?**

Dye was born in Oskaloosa, Iowa, in 1918. As a kid, he lived in St. Joseph, MO. The Depression was still on, and Edison and his mom moved to southern California, where an uncle had a good job. The kid studied Aeronautical Engineering in college, and built a hot rod that he raced on El Mirage dry lake. During the war years, he built B-24s in Texas.

He wanted to see the world, and set up a motorcycle tour business. The first destination he offered was the Isle of Man TT. In the UK he became aware of motocross, which was still virtually unheard of back home. (In the 1950s, Americans raced 'scrambles', on tracks laid out on much smoother terrain; motocross featured jumps, steeper hills, mud and ruts.)

On his first trip to Europe, Dye bought a 125cc Zundapp scrambler. He sold it back home to defray expenses. On the next trip, he met with Husqvarna, and talked the company into making him the U.S. distributor. It probably wasn't that hard, since there was no interest in motocross in the U.S. at all. Husky sent him back with two bikes, one to ride, and one he could take around to show dealers.

Day 65 – Malcolm comes on board

Dye's first marketing break came when he got Malcolm Smith to test a Husky. Malcolm concluded it would be better in the desert than his Greeves. Dealers were impressed with the machines, too; Dye sold 100 of them in the first year, always trying to ensure that they got into the best local racers' hands.

The next year, Dye brought Lars Larsson over to stage a bunch of demonstration races. At that point, there were still no real motocross tracks here. They'd lay out a course on whatever natural terrain they could find. If there was hill or a gully on the edge of a local scrambles course, so much the better; they would race through that. The second year, Dye sold 500 Huskies. The next year he brought over Torsten Hallman, and sold 1,000.

Day 66 – Then, Dye had a falling-out with the AMA. (Surprise, surprise.)

In 1967, he brought over Hallman, Joel Robert, Roger DeCoster, Arne Kring, Ake Johnson, and Dave Bickers. His 'demonstration' races had evolved into the Inter-Am race series, pitting fast-improving Americans against top European riders (the series took place in the fall, after World Championship.)

The AMA had little interest in motocross until they saw the crowds at Dye's events. Then, the organization began counter-promoting against him, running the 'Trans-AMA' series. They told track owners that if they worked with Dye, they'd be denied future AMA events. Perhaps to avoid a lawsuit, the AMA then allowed Dye to promote some of their events.

Dye's final falling-out with the AMA came in 1974. He canceled a Trans-AMA race in St. Louis, because of rain. Dye knew that if the weather was bad, the fans would stay home leaving him on the hook for purse money. Canceling the event was a dick move on Dye's part, and it gave the AMA they excuse they needed to blackball him.

Edison Dye was a sad old man before he was finally acknowledged for his role in the development of American motocross. He died on his 89th birthday.

Day 67 – **U.S. World Champions**

The proof in the American motocross pudding came in 1981—about 15 years after Dye's first Inter-Am race—when the U.S. won the Motocross of Nations event in Bielstein, Germany. The MXoN pits four-man national teams against each other in mixed displacement categories. It's been held every year since 1947.

In those first few decades, the MXoN was won by the UK, Belgium, and Sweden. But once the first full generation of American riders had grown up in the post-Dye era, the U.S. was unstoppable.

The first winning U.S. team was made up of Donnie Hansen, Danny Laporte, Johnny O'Mara and Chuck Sun.

The Americans proved it was no fluke by winning the next 12 years in a row.

Day 68 – Weirdly compelling motorcycle movie: *The Born Losers*

This 1967 movie was produced, directed, and stars Tom Laughlin. It was the first appearance of his character 'Billy Jack', who reappeared in *The Legend of Billy Jack* in 1971.

The Born Losers is no *Billy Jack*. But, the people who love it see it as a subtle allegory expressing Laughlin's opposition to the Vietnam War. That interpretation passed over the heads of most people who saw when it was first released, but it has to be one of the very best of the '60s bikesploitation flicks. The movie also stars Laughlin's real-life wife, Dolores Taylor.

Cool fact: Laughlin starred in Robert Altman's 1957 film *The Delinquents*, playing a character that could easily have been a young Billy Jack. It's as if he really only played one role during his whole acting career.

•

Sons of Anarchy

'Sons of Anarchy' creator Kurt Sutter researched real motorcycle gangs before creating FX Network's most popular show. Sutter updated the idea of returning veterans forming outlaw bike gangs by making the founder of the gang a disgruntled Vietnam vet.

Day 69 – "Advertising? We don't need no stinkin' advertising!"

According to *Advertising Age*, the producers of the show approached Harley-Davidson with the idea of sponsoring the first episode, perhaps commercial-free. Harley's Chief Marketing Officer, Mark-Hans Richer, suggested instead that the company provide all the motorcycles the club members would ride on the show.

"There are things that happen on the show that we wouldn't endorse as a corporation," Richer told Ad Age. "But the spirit is very authentic—it's about the bond between individuals."

Ad Age rated the deal between H-D and SAMCRO as one of the top-10 product placements of all time. The motorcycle maker denies that it has ever paid money to have its bikes appear.

Day 70 – Seven seasons of free publicity (and eternal reruns)

If that product placement claim is true, Harley deserves extra credit for not insisting on brand-new bikes. Most of the bikes are Dynas that were a few years old when the show first started shooting. One old member was portrayed as riding a Tri-Glide trike that was modified to carry his oxygen bottle. (If Harley-Davidson's customer base gets any older, the company should make that an option.)

'Opie', a character killed off in Season 5, was occasionally seen working on a Harley Panhead. The motorcycle seen inside the clubhouse—in the show, it's supposed to have been the club founder's personal ride—was built on a '48

Panhead wishbone frame. The fuel tanks are '51 Panhead items. The springer front end and motor are '46 Knucklehead.

Day 71 – It ain't no *Downton Abbey* (but…)

By the series' end, Jackson 'Jax' Teller (portrayed by actor Charlie Hunnam) has become the club president.

Hunnam's breakout role was as a gay teenager in *'Queer as Folk'*. And, he once admitted that in a break from shooting the biker series, he binge-watched *Downton Abbey* to catch up. That said, Hunnam's real-life father was a 'gangster' and scrap-metal dealer, so it's possible the SAMCRO character came easy to the English actor.

For what it's worth, in the interests of realism, Sutter made sure that all his actors could actually ride motorcycles. Those who didn't ride were given lessons. Hunnam really took to it, and was often seen riding around L.A. on the same Harley that appeared in the show.

Ironically, the one cast member who didn't like motorcycles—and rode only when the script called for it and cameras were rolling—was Ron Perlman who, as Clay Barrow, was supposed to be a murderous badass.

Day 72 – Shakespeare is shaking his head

The cliché was that *Sons of Anarchy* was "*Hamlet* on Harleys". Kurt Sutter downplayed that idea, but admitted there was something to it.

According to the website askmen.com, *"Clay (Ron Perlman) is based on the role of King Claudius, who murdered his own brother (Hamlet's father) to win the*

*throne and marry Queen Gertrude (Hamlet's mother).
Clay marries Gemma (Katey Sagal), the Gertrude figure,
and gains control of The Sons of Anarchy, which her dead
husband used to run. Jax is Hamlet. His confusion over the
SOA lifestyle is like Hamlet's melancholy about the
kingdom. While Jax communicates with his father by
reading his journal, Hamlet literally speaks with the ghost
of his father."*

Biggest motorcycle companies you've never heard of

Harley-Davidson still has the most recognized motorcycle
brand in the world, and (for now) has the highest revenues
of any motorcycle manufacturer (or division, if you want
to compare sales of Honda or BMW motorcycles, for
example.)

But there are companies—including companies you've
never heard of—that actually sell more motorcycles than
Harley. If you count scooters and mopeds, motorcycles
still outnumber cars in many developing economies. It's
safe to say that if you ever find yourself in Sepang, or
Bombay, or Hanoi, you'll see a bunch of brands Americans
are not familiar with.

The rap on a lot of these bike is that they're cheap but
crappy and will never catch on in the U.S. or European
markets. But of course, that's what your dad or grandfather
said about Japanese bikes in the early '60s.

Here's a cheat sheet for some of the top Chinese, Korean,
and Indian brands, and an educated guess about which
ones you might see enter the U.S. market in coming
years...

Day 73 – **Lifan (China)**

In 1992, Yin Mingshan was an unemployable political dissident in the city of Chongqing—a sprawling municipality at the confluence of the Yangtze and Jialing rivers in southwestern China.

With few other options, Yin started a motorcycle repair shop with a handful of employees. Less than 10 years later, Lifan (the word means 'great sail') became the first Chinese motorcycle brand sold in Japan.

Americans tend to think of China as a low-cost manufacturing country, but Lifan has learned that it can build bikes even cheaper elsewhere. The company has factories in Thailand, Turkey, and Vietnam. In total, it currently builds about 1.8 million motorcycles per year.

If you've really been paying attention, you may have spotted a Lifan or two on U.S. roads. The company attempted to establish an American

distributor a few years ago, but it was not prepared for that first foray into the U.S. market.

In the meantime, Lifan's set up a strategic partnership with MV Agusta, which may lead to improved styling, if nothing else.

Day 74 – **Loncin (China)**

Loncin is another Chinese motorcycle company headquartered in Chongqing. The founder, Tu Jianhua, started Loncin Holdings Company in the early '80s, after he was injured on his previous job, at a state-run coal mine. By 1993, he made gasoline engines. Loncin launched its first complete motorcycle in 1999. In 2002, the company cut the ribbon on a new R&D center.

Now, Loncin manufactures over a million bikes a year, at factories in Chongqing, Zhejiang, and Guandong.

If you've traveled in Mexico or Argentina and seen Italika- or Zanella-brand motorcycles, there's an excellent chance they were actually made by Loncin. The company has also acquired Amino, an Egyptian brand that sells throughout Africa.

The company is capable of top-quality manufacturing. Loncin manufactures whole motors for BMW motorcycles in a part of the factory under direct supervision by BMW engineers. It also supplies components for GM, VW, and BMW cars.

Day 75 – **Zongshen (China)**

Zuo Zongshen is another guy who started out with a small repair shop in Chongqing—which by now you realize is the epicenter of the Chinese motorcycle industry!

His company has grown to produce over a million bikes a year, but more it has more than sheer size going for it. Zongshen is more vertically integrated than most Chinese motorcycle companies, which allows it to maintain better quality control. Zongshen's also built an impressive R&D center, and (shades of Soichiro Honda!) places a high value on racing experience. Although most of the time when 'Zongshen' goes racing they're actually racing other people's motorcycles. For example, when Zongshen entered the FIM World Endurance Championship, it did so with a Suzuki GSX-R. Still, Zongshen engineers learned plenty from the experience.

Zongshen supplies motorcycles sold as Motohispanias in Spain and AKT in Colombia. The company's biggest overseas investment is in Brazil, where it has acquired the Kasinski brand. And now it's here in the U.S.: If you've seen a CSC Cyclone 250cc 'adventure'-style motorcycle—something that resembles a baby BMW GS—it's made by Zongshen, and sells for about ¼ the cost of a real BMW.

Day 76 – **Jialing is the oldest Chinese motorcycle company**

Most of the biggest Chinese motorcycle companies emerged after the Communist Party began to encourage entrepreneurial activity and endorsed a degree of capitalism. But the most established Chinese brand, Jialing, is a part of the state-owned South China Industries Group.

This company has roots in the manufacture of guns and military equipment, and goes back to before Mao led the Communist revolution in China.

A number of classic Honda engine designs have been shamelessly copied by low-cost Chinese producers, but Honda has formed official joint ventures with Jialing since the early '80s. It was one of the first Chinese companies to tackle a larger displacement bike when it released the JH600 'dual sport' model, which is often used by Chinese police.

Day 77 – **The government throws a wrench into domestic sales**

All the Chinese companies have been hurt by big Chinese cities banning motorcycles outright.

If you occasionally feel persecuted as a motorcyclist in the U.S., take heart in the fact that at least you don't live in China, where beginning around 2007, several big cities summarily banned motorcycles. Hundreds of thousands of Chinese motorcycle owners were forced to either sell their bikes to peasants in the countryside, or turn them into to the police in exchange for a token payment.

The crazy thing about the bans is, the decisions were made with almost no explanation. Sure, Chinese traffic is terrible, and air quality in Chinese cities is ghastly; motorcycles contributed to those problems, but rather than enforce stricter licensing, traffic laws, and emissions standards, they've just banned motorcycles, forcing people to sell what is often their most valuable asset—usually at a big loss. One of the reasons officials cite is a rash of purse-snatchings and strong-arm robberies in which motorcycles have been used as getaway vehicles.

Day 78 – **Hero is a villain to Erik Buell's fans**

Hero MotoCorp is the largest motorcycle maker in India, and it has nearly half the huge Indian domestic market.

Hero traces its roots to a bicycle company run by four brothers from Pakistan. They built Hero Cycles into India's largest bicycle company and then, in 1984, formed Hero Honda Motors—a joint venture that gave Honda easier access to the tightly controlled Indian domestic market. The Hero Group bought Honda's shares when it decided to get out of the joint venture in 2010.

If American riders know Hero at all, it's usually because the company was briefly a sponsor of Erik Buell's racing team and (even more briefly) an investor in Buell's company after it was cut loose by Harley-Davidson.

Day 79 – **Motorcycles mean independence**

Bajaj Auto Group, despite that non-moto name, is one of the world's largest motorcycle manufacturers.

The company traces its roots back to Jamnalal Bajaj, who was born in 1889. Bajaj is a famous figure in India. He was an early follower of Mahatma Gandhi, and fought for India's independence from Britain. Part of Gandhi's philosophy was that India needed to regain not just political independence but economic self-sufficiency. Bajaj was inspired by that idea, and sought to turn India into an industrial nation that was not dependent on Britain for manufactured goods.

Bajaj's industrial empire expanded in 1944, when Bajaj Auto began importing motorbikes. It started manufacturing its own bikes in 1960. By 1995, it had produced 10 million of them. KTM and Husqvarna have also outsourced a lot of motorcycle assembly to Bajaj.

Bajaj Auto Group is still a family business, managed by the founder's grandson. The family are major philanthropists in India.

Day 80 – TVS (No, that's not an obscure cable channel)

The third big Indian company is TVS, which produces a range of scooters, mopeds, small motorcycles.

TVS is active on the Indian racing scene, where there are fiercely competitive classes for mopeds and scooters, as well as small-displacement motorcycles. They've scored class wins in the Raid de Himalaya (sort of a Paris-Dakar with high mountains instead of the Sahara as the challenge.)

Although TVS fancies itself as a 'sporty' company, most of it's products are utilitarian. Of those, the most weird-and-wonderful is a three-wheeled vehicle called the 'King'. It looks like the front of a scooter that's been grafted onto the back of a minivan. You want one. I'm not kidding, you really do. They make several models adapted for carrying cargo or up to four people and even offer it with a 436cc single-cylinder diesel motor that produces about 7 horsepower.

Day 81 – Honda trains its competitors

Honda, by now, probably considers itself a sort of global charity, dedicated to teaching people in developing economies how to build their own motorcycles and, ultimately, compete with Honda for sales.

That's how KYMCO got its start, in Taiwan. The name's in all caps, because it's an acronym for Kwang Yang Motor Co., Ltd.

Kymco was one of the first 'offshore' parts suppliers for Honda, and the first of those Honda relationships to sour when it decided it wanted to sell components to other companies and then, in 1970, compete in the marketplace with a scooter of its own. Now, the company has factories in several other locations including Jakarta, Indonesia.

The company is still forming strategic alliances with better-known brands. It has often supplied whole engines for some of the smaller BMW motorcycles, and now supplies the small 'range extender' motor used in the BMW i3 hybrid automobile.

Day 82 – **Daelim**

Daelim Motors has had a sketchy history in the U.S., importing a few scooters and then abandoning its American operation in about 2007. But it's a thriving company, with a line-up of scooters and small motorcycles and a presence on the vibrant Korean scooter-racing scene.

Daelim Motors is a subsidiary of Daelim Industrial Co., which is a 'chaebol'—that's a huge, diversified industrial conglomerate. A handful of chaebols account for most of Korea's manufacturing industry. They're unlike any American company in the range of businesses they're involved in. You might not be surprised to learn that a scooter company also supplies motors and components to the auto industry, but Daelim's parent company also designs and builds oil refineries and powerplants, and operates a chain of luxury hotels.

Day 83 – **Hyosung**

Hyosung is the best-known Korean motorcycle brand in the U.S., though consumer acceptance of Korean motorcycles is somewhere in between that of the country's cars (which have now reached mainstream acceptance) and the country's pop stars (still an acquired taste.)

Hyosung Motors was formed in 1979 by another one of those chaebol conglomerates, to produce Suzuki motorcycles under license. In 2003, however, Hyosung Motors and Machinery was spun off to become its own company.

A few years later, it was acquired by another Korean company, S&T Group ('Science and Technology'). The new owners renamed the motorcycle division 'S&T Motors' although they continued to sell motorcycles branded 'Hyosung'.

In 2014, the Hyosung motorcycle brand was acquired again, this time by Kolao Holdings; a company that distributes Korean cars in Southeast Asia. Kolao's motorcycle business came to be known as KR Motors. Hyosung motorcycles are still sold in the U.S., by KRM America. The company aspires to be the Kia of motorcycles.

•

Day 84 – **Worth Knowing: Lane Splitting**

Lane splitting (aka 'filtering') is perhaps the best thing about riding a motorcycle in congested traffic. In Europe, filtering is considered such an essential skill that it is part of your license practical test. In some Asian countries, there are two stop lines at each red light; one line for cars and another one a few yards ahead, so that motorcycles and scooters can filter to the front of the line and race ahead when the light turns green.

Sadly (at least at the time of this writing) lane splitting is permitted in only one American state: California. In other states, motorcyclists have argued that it's actually safer – for motorcycles – than sitting in stop and go traffic; we've argued that motorcycles are more likely to overheat when stopped for long periods; and we've pointed out that when motorcycles can travel in between lanes, everyone gets where they're going a little bit faster. All to no avail.

Until very recently, lane splitting was not even expressly permitted in California; it just wasn't expressly banned. So every day thousands of California commuters rode to work in a 'gray area' – both legally and because it's the color of asphalt. California motorcyclists were divided on the recent move to write a law specifically permitting lane splitting. But motorcyclists in the rest of the U.S. should take heart. California's set an example; it should be easier for other states to follow suit.

•

Everyone had to start somewhere

Even the most established motorcycle companies started somewhere—and it was often making products that have no relationship to motorcycles. Know why Yamaha's logo looks like three crossed tuning forks? Because the company got its start making pianos, and only made the move into motorbikes when postwar Japan needed cheap, reliable transportation more than it needed music.

Here are few interesting origin stories…

Day 85 – **Ducati**

Ducati started out in the radio business. In 1926, *Società Scientifica Radio Brevetti Ducati* was founded by Antonio Cavalieri Ducati and his three sons, Adriano, Marcello, and Bruno. At first they concentrated on making vacuum tubes and condensers, but within a decade they'd opened a factory in the Borgo Panigale district of Bologna, where they made radios and a few other small household appliances. The Ducati motorcycle factory's still in the same neighborhood.

Needless to say, the radio factory was a high profile target for Allied bombers during the war, but the company survived comparatively unscathed.

Meanwhile, there was a great need for cheap transportation after the war. SIATA, a company across the country in Turin, developed a gasoline motor that could be attached to an ordinary bicycle. It was known as the Cucciolo ('little puppy'). When demand outstripped their ability to manufacture it, they sought a partner with a bigger factory.

Ducati stepped in, and within a few years, they were manufacturing thousands of Cucciolo motors (or is that 'Cuccioli'?) per month. By the early 1950s, Ducati had designed its own complete motorbike, still on basic bicycle running gear but incorporating a three-speed gearbox.

That was officially known as the Model 48, though riders still called them 'Cucciolo'. Soon after Ducati started making entire motorbikes, the founders split their business into two separate companies, Ducati Meccanica SpA and Ducati Elettronica, which in turn became Ducati Energia the eighties.

Ducati Energia is still in business. It makes, among other things, wind power generators.

Day 86 – So, Ichiro, what are you going to do now?

Soichiro Honda was a self-taught auto mechanic. In 1937, he borrowed money to start a piston-ring manufacturing business, which failed because of the poor quality of his products. Honda then attended engineering school, although he never graduated. He completed his education by visiting factories (especially Toyota factories) around Japan, where he peppered engineers with questions.

Honda's piston-ring factory ('Tokai Seiki' means 'Eastern Sea Precision Machine') was then capable of meeting Toyota's quality control standards, but it was flattened in the war. He sold the wreckage to Toyota, and used the proceeds to fund the Honda Technical Research Institute in 1946. That sounds a lot more grandiose than it was; it was 12 guys working in a 170 square-foot hut.

Honda bought up hundreds of war-surplus gasoline generator motors. They had originally been designed as a power supply for military radios. Honda and his team converted them to power bicycles—much like those first Ducatis. When he ran out of surplus motors, he created his own small motor.

In 1949, the Honda Technical Research Institute was liquidated and Soichiro Honda sunk the proceeds (about $5,000 in today's terms) into the Honda Motor Co. The first complete Honda motorcycle, with both a Honda frame and motor, was the 1949 D-Type. When Honda fired it up for the first time, one of his employees shouted, "It's like a dream!" That was the first Honda Dream.

Day 87 – **Suzuki**

Can you stand one more story about a post-WWII clip-on motor for bicycles? If you can't, skip one day ahead. Otherwise, read on to learn that Michio Suzuki formed the Suzuki Loom Works in 1909. The company made weaving equipment that was highly regarded in the Japanese silk industry.

In the late 1930s, Suzuki felt that his company would benefit from some other product line. He funded the R&D needed to produce several small car prototypes that were advanced for their day. Unfortunately, civilian car production was deemed 'non-essential' during the war years, so he was unable to get the materials needed to put a vehicle into production.

After the war, Suzuki decided a cheaper mode of transportation made more sense as a commercial product, so the company sold bicycles equipped with a 36cc one-horsepower motor it called the 'Power Free'. A clever sprocket arrangement allowed users to pedal without the motor turning at all (if they'd run out of gas, for example) or run the motor and let the pedals freewheel. A third setting allowed the rider to provide pedal assistance to the motor.

The company is still run by a guy named Suzuki, but interestingly, he's what's called an 'adopted son-in-law' in Japan. If a Japanese family has no male heirs, a man who marries their daughter can take on that family name. Daughters often have no say in the choice of these husbands; they're basically 'hired' for their qualifications in running the family business.

Day 88 – **The Treaty of Versailles' connection to motorcycling**

Every BMW fan knows that the 'roundel'—that blue-and-white logo, was meant to evoke a spinning airplane propeller. But do you know *why* the company switched from aircraft motors to motorcycles?

After the First World War, the 1919 Versailles Armistice Treaty prevented German industry from manufacturing anything that might have a military use. That forced the Rapp Motorenwerke—an aircraft engine plant in Munich —to reinvent itself.

The founders first retooled their plant to produce crude truck and boat engines that were permitted under the terms of the treaty. Germany negotiated somewhat loosened restrictions, and by 1923 the company was permitted to manufacture motorcycles. Even that very first BMW, the R32, is clearly recognizable as a 'beemer' and bears a distinct similarity to some of the current models.

Before WWII, BMW returned to making aircraft engines. The company was a key player in the Nazi war effort. Nowadays, the company is careful to de-emphasize the fact that much factory work was done by the inmates of the nearby Dachau concentration camp.

Day 89 – **No wonder they produced the 'Shooting Star'**

By the time BSA had acquired Triumph, it was the largest motorcycle company in the world. But it got it's start as the Birmingham Small Arms company. (If you look closely, that triangular BSA logo is made up of three rifles.

In 1861, a group of gunsmiths launched a new factory with advanced machinery to mass-produce weapons. Within a few years, BSA had diversified. It's first non-firearm effort was the manufacture of the Otto Dicycle, under license. The Dicycle had two large bicycle wheels, arranged side-by-side. If you look at a picture of one, you'll wonder how in hell anyone maintained fore-and-aft stability.

Short answer, they didn't. Which is why the dicycle flopped (both frontwards and backwards.)

The invention of the Rover 'safety bicycle'—with the basic 'diamond' frame that's still common—made bicycles far more practical. By 1908, BSA was making its own version, and the first 3½ hp motorcycle was shown in 1910.

•

**Guys love things that go 'bang'
as much as things that go 'vroom'**

By now, you've realized that the history of 20th century manufacturing is closely tied to the history of 20th c. warfare. That is not a problem for motorcyclists, because generally speaking guys like things that go bang as much as they like things that go vroom.

Royal Enfield famously advertised, "Made like a gun, goes like a bullet". And indeed the Enfield Bullet survives as a motorcycle to this day. Here are some of the other motorcycle companies that make (or made) firearms, and some gun makers that make (or made) motorcycles.

Day 90 – **This explains Husqvarna's logo**

Husqvarna got its start in the late 1600s, when a gun maker set up a small factory near a waterfall, so the factory equipment could be driven by water-wheel.

Husky made rifles and shotguns for over 300 years. The company diversified into other products like sewing machines and motorcycles, but kept its 'gun sight' logo. Gun collectors still prize the HVA bolt action rifle, which was Husqvarna's take on the ubiquitous Mauser 98 action.

The Swedes sold their motorcycle division to Cagiva in 1987, and the brand was sold again, to KTM, in 2013. They've also stopped making rifles, but the tooling for their premium bolt-action rifles was acquired by an Italian armorer named Antonio Zoli. He still sells them under the AZ1900 name. There's about a six-month wait.

Day 91 – **Momma knew best**

In 1911, Teresa Benelli was an Italian widow with a problem: creating some kind of stable family income and employment for her six sons. Her idea was to invest in a garage, where her mechanically-inclined progeny could earn a living repairing bicycles, motorbikes, and cars.

During the First World War, the brothers became increasingly self-sufficient; they just made any parts they needed. In 1919, the built their first motor from scratch; it was a 75cc two-stroke. By 1921, they'd shown their first entire motorbike.

In the early years, Antonio 'Tonino' Benelli, the youngest brother, won several Italian championships on their 175 overhead-cam single. Then, the marque achieved much wider attention with a win at the 1939 Lightweight TT.

The Benelli works was severely damaged in WWII, but the factory team was back in the World Championship for 1950, and won several 250cc-class titles including the last 250cc championship for a four-stroke motor, under Kel Carruthers in 1969.

The brothers were also avid hunters, so in 1967 they created a subsidiary, Benelli Armi, and hired Bruno Civolani who invented the 'Inertia Driven' mechanism. Within a few years, their factory in Urbino was producing a thousand shotguns a day.

Meanwhile, the motorcycle side of the business was increasingly dependent on U.S. sales through Montgomery Ward, and they were hit hard by the rising quality and performance of Japanese imports. In 1973 the motorcycle business was sold to Alejandro de Tomaso, and it's changed hands a couple of times since. The brand is currently under Chinese control.

Benelli Armi remained largely intact after being sold to Beretta in 1983. The Benelli Ethos was named 2014 Shotgun of the Year by Guns & Ammo.

Day 92 – **Joel Robert bounced Czechs**

In 1919, an armaments factory opened in South Bohemia (now the Czech Republic) called Jihočeská zbrojovka.

After a merger, it became the Czech Armament Works, known by its Czech initials CZ. By 1932, the armament maker had branched into bicycles and motorbikes. It became the biggest motorcycle maker in Czechoslovakia, and supplied chains to other bicycle and motorcycle makers.

During the Communist era, CZ was merged with another motorcycle maker, Jawa. Along with MZ (in East Germany), CZ carried the Communist banner in World Championship racing. CZs scored podium finishes in Grand Prix road racing, before the factory shifted emphasis to motocross to reduce racing expenses. Joel Robert won several 250cc World Championships for his Commie taskmasters through the 1960s.

Meanwhile, CZ continued to produce arms and (curiously, considering the political climate) exported millions of pistols to the west. A no less fervent red baiter than Jeff Cooper once described the CZ75 as the best 9mm pistol he'd ever handled. The contemporary CZ P09 is considered to be a solid, versatile handgun bargain.

Day 93 – **No FN kidding**

The FN-FAL rifle was one of the most battle-proven weapons of the 20th century.

'FN' stands for Fabrique Nationale d'Armes de Guerre, a weapons factory near Liege, Belgium. The company has an American connection, too; it was John Moses Browning's most loyal licensee, reproducing his designs for over a century.

FN is still well known to marksmen; it's Ballista sniper rifle was considered for use by the U.S. Armed Forces. But few American motorcyclists remember that before the First World War, FN also made some of the most sophisticated motorcycles. The company was best known for elegant, shaft-driven four cylinder bikes.

The first FN Four was unveiled at the 1905 Paris auto show. At the time, it was claimed to be the fastest production motorcycle, with a top speed of 40 miles per hour. The Four was good enough to remain in production until 1923. FN produced motorcycles into the 1960s.

Day 94 – **The choice of domestic terrorists**

Iver Johnson was a Norwegian gunsmith who emigrated to the United States and settled in Worcester, MA at the height of the Civil War. He worked as a local gunsmith and freelanced as a firearms designer for bigger firms. Eventually he merged his business with another gunsmith named Martin Bye. Those two received a number of joint patents for firearms, until Johnson bought Bye's interest in the partnership.

Johnson's company was known for a time as Johnson's Arms and Cycle Works. It caught the beginning of the American bicycle boom in 1891, sponsoring well-known racers.

Iver died of tuberculosis in 1895 but his sons took over the business, branching into motorcycles in 1907. By that time, the factory had moved to Fitchburg, MA.

Iver Johnson motorcycles were technologically advanced for their day. The company made motorcycles until 1916. Then, management decided to return to their core competency (weapons.)

I suppose the big asterisk, when it comes to Iver Johnson's firearms history, is that William McKinley, Franklin Roosevelt, and Bobby Kennedy were all shot with Iver Johnson pistols.

Day 95 – **The motorcycle that won the west?**

If there's an iconic American gun brand, it's Winchester. But few gun *or* motorcycle historians remember that for a brief time, Winchester also sold motorcycles.

Winchester was one of the first companies to embrace the idea of brand extension, contracting with other companies to supply 'Winchester' branded products from baseballs to bikes.

The Edwin F. Merry company, of San Francisco, supplied Winchester with 200 single cylinder motorcycles, similar to early Harley-Davidson or Indian singles, in 1910. It was advertised at $160. The Merry company is still in business, and is still a distributor of bicycle components.

Only one of those 200 motorcycles is known to have survived. That example sold for $580,000 in 2014.

Day 96 – **Miyata was Japan's first motorcycle manufacturer**

In 1881, Eisuke Miyata opened his gunsmithy in Shiba. A few years later, a foreigner asked him to repair his bicycle. Miyata's son then used the firm's barrel-making equipment to create bicycle tubing and his own built-from-scratch bike.

By 1900, the Japanese market was being flooded with foreign firearms, and Miyata shifted its attention to bicycles only. The company is often cited as the first one to use triple-butted tubing.

In 1913, the Tokyo police department approached Miyata with a request for motorcycles. The firm bought a

Triumph, and made a faithful—if expensive—copy. It was dubbed the 'Asahi'. That first effort was far too expensive to appeal to the general public, but the police used them. The Asahi police bike is sometimes described as the first 'mass-produced' Japanese motorcycle.

Asahi produced a nice-looking 'AA' model in 1933, which the Society of Automotive Engineers of Japan included in their list of 240 Landmarks of Japanese Automotive Technology. According to the eminent motorcycle historian Erwin Tragatsch, Asahi made bikes in postwar Japan, from 1953-'65.

Although Miyata bicycles are not common in the U.S., they're still popular in the rest of the world.

Day 97 – **A web site worth knowing: Bike-urious**

www.bike-urious.com is a Los Angeles-based web site put up by Abhi Eswarappa, whose business card reads, 'Director of Shenanigans'. You might guess from this that he doesn't take himself too seriously. At first, he was one of those guys reposting interesting 'Bike for sale' ads from Craigslist and Ebay, but as his audience has grown, so have has the range of his subject matter.

In his own words…

Implying I have and editorial philosophy is being generous, but the basic idea is that I just feature bikes I think are interesting for any reason - even if that reason is the bike was horrible. I don't really enjoy creating the 'bike for sale' posts any more because I don't get to ride them, just stare at them from afar and write about them. What good is being a kid in a candy shop if I can't eat anything?

So I also spend a lot of time trying to convince companies to give me press bikes!

To me it's all about showing how much fun motorcycles can be, no matter the specific brand or model you might be on.

•

Everyone needs a best Bud

The most famous Winchester rifle is probably the cut down .44-40 Model 1892 carried by Steve McQueen in the television series 'Wanted: Dead of Alive' from 1958- '61.

That prop gun was designed by Kenny 'Von Dutch' Howard. Yes, *that* Von Dutch. Now, he's remembered as a pinstriper and custom motorcycle guy, but he was also a gunsmith and knife-maker.

Von Dutch and McQueen were tight, but Steve's best pal was Bud Ekins. Bud was a stuntman, Triumph dealer, and Steve's racing mentor.

Day 98 – Meeting broads was job #1

In the beginning, Terence Steven McQueen was just another punk in 'Boy's Republic' — a reform school in the dusty farming town of Chino, California. He joined the Marine Corps, where he trained as a mechanic. His military record was not spotless, but he was granted an honorable discharge. Under the provisions of the G.I. Bill, Uncle Sam paid his tuition at the elite Actor's Studio in New York City. He didn't expect to become a star, he just thought acting school would be a good place to meet broads. He rode around New York's 'Hell's Kitchen' neighborhood on a Harley 45.

Day 99 – **A budding interest in desert racing**

Steve never had any interest in racing until he met James Sherwin 'Bud' Ekins, a stunt man who also owned an L.A. Triumph dealership. He was the 'go to' guy whenever a movie or TV production needed bikes. Besides carrying an inventory of new Triumphs, he had warehouses full of older and weirder stuff. Studios didn't usually buy motorcycles for productions; they preferred to lease bikes that Bud supplied, along with what amounted to a service contract to keep them in running order for the duration of the shoot.

When a show needed a motorcycle stunt, Bud was often paid twice, once for providing the bike, and then again for the 'gag' (that's what stunt professionals call a stunt.) It was very profitable, although Bud 'reinvested' a lot of that money in racing, parties, and girls.

Bud was one of the fastest off-road racers of his day. He cut 10 minutes off the race-record time at the Catalina Grand Prix in 1955. A few years later, he finished the Big Bear enduro half an hour ahead of the second-place rider.

Ekins became a mentor and 'older brother' character to McQueen—who otherwise trusted almost no one.

Day 100 – **Bud won an ISDT Gold Medal in 1962**

Bud Ekins is perhaps most famous as the guy who doubled for Steve McQueen in the famous jump scene in 'The Great Escape'. During filming outside Munich in 1962, the entire shoot practically went on hiatus, because Bud had also entered the International Six Days Trial which was taking place nearby at Garmisch-Partenkirchen.

They could've shot around the absence of Bud, but Steve and a bunch of the other guys involved insisted on going to cheer Bud on to a gold-medal finish.

Day 101 – **Steve McQueen, proud nationalist (and party animal)**

Bud was one of the few Yanks capable of winning an ISDT Gold Medal. That was certainly *not* a description of Steve, who was enthusiastic but not particularly talented.

In spite of the fact that the ISDT was over Steve's head, he concocted a plan to enter the first American team, in 1964. (Individual American riders had entered previously, notably John Penton as well as Bud, but there'd never been an official four-man national team.)

The ISDT's often called 'The Olympics of Motorcycling' and one of the pseudo-Olympic aspects is that it begins with a flag ceremony in which four-man national teams parade their flag. In 1964, the presence of the Stars and Stripes was even more noteworthy, because the event was held in Ehrfurt, East Germany, on the Communist side of the Iron Curtain.

The American team was comprised of Bud, Steve, Dave Ekins (Bud's younger brother) and Cliff Coleman (who worked in the movie business, too.) Steve insisted on blazers and ties during the official ceremony.

Steve arranged for Triumph to supply them with new motorcycles. McQueen was a notorious tightwad, which made paying for the trip to Europe a problem. A big French magazine, Paris Match, came to the rescue. The magazine wanted to run a feature story about McQueen to coincide with the French premiere of 'Love With The Proper Stanger'. Steve said he'd come over, but that the magazine had to pay for a few bodyguards to travel with him. The 'bodyguards' were Bud, Dave, and Cliff, along with Elmer Valentine who ran the Whiskey a Go Go disco in Los Angeles. (Does it sound like a serious party trip?)

Day 102 – **"How's my face?"**

The race itself was not a success for either Steve or Bud. The Americans were in contention for the Silver Vase for a couple of days, but any hopes of a result were dashed on the third. McQueen, last on the road, had to dodge spectators who were beginning to move around on the course. He'd already fallen and needed stitches in his face, which was a frightening prospect for a movie star. Anyway, the next crash bent his fork and his race was kaput.

"Steve was fast," Dave Ekins once told me. "But he started racing too late to ever really be relaxed on the bike. And to do well in a long event, you have to be both fast and relaxed."

That same day, Bud crashed and broke an ankle, although he remounted and finished without losing a point. After discussing their prospects over a few Scotches that evening, Bud decided that he, too, was done.

It probably didn't feel that way in the moment, but the '64 event was rated an easy one by ISDT veterans. Dave Ekins and Cliff Coleman won individual Gold medals.

Day 103 – *40 Summers Ago… Hollywood Behind the Iron Curtain*

Johnson Motors, the west coast Triumph distributor, sent a film crew to document Steve's ISDT. But the film was shelved when the team's results proved disappointing.

Years later, a book was compiled that included a number of stills from that lost 16mm film, as well as images shot for Paris Match. It was published with the cooperation of the McQueen estate. *40 Summers Ago… Hollywood Behind the Iron Curtain* was originally sold for $50, it's now out of print and copies trade on eBay for as much as $50—proof that Steve still deserves his status as 'The King of Cool'.

Day 104 – **Alias 'Harvey Mushman'. Or worse…**

By the mid- '60s, McQueen was one of the world's most recognizable stars. Although he certainly didn't mind the attention he got from female fans, he enjoyed the anonymity that came with wearing a crash helmet and goggles.

He often entered District 37 desert races under the alias of 'Harvey Mushman'. According to Bobby Foxworth, who was a mechanic at Bud's Triumph dealership and frequent riding buddy, Steve also occasionally went by a ruder alias: 'Haywood Jablomie'.

Even though he never sought to publicize his own racing efforts, McQueen agreed to appear in Bruce Brown's epic motorcycle racing documentary, 'On Any Sunday', because he knew that if the poster included the words, "Starring Steve McQueen" the film would get a major theatrical release.

Day 105 – **When life gives you Le Mans...**

Although we remember McQueen as a motorcycle guy, one of his great life quests was to make an epic, highly realistic film of the 24-hour sports car race at Le Mans. That 1971 film, *Le Mans*, was actually filmed during the real 1970 Le Mans race. The original plan had been for Steve to enter the race with Jackie Stewart as a co-driver, but their entry was turned down. In spite of that, McQueen's Porsche 908/2 (which he raced at Sebring) was entered in the race, and doubled as a camera car. The reason the racing seems realistic is, those scenes were shot from the track, during the actual 24 Hours of Le Mans.

Unfortunately, that attention to detail did not really extend as far as the plot or dialog. The movie was a critical and commercial failure.

Day 106 – **Every movie ends**

After 'Towering Inferno', McQueen might've been the highest-paid actor in the world, but his reputation increasingly resulted in directors and producers casting other stars, even in roles that had been written with him in mind.

In 1978, he developed a persistent cough. It was identified as mesothelioma, a cancer commonly associated with asbestos exposure. McQueen may have been exposed while serving in the military; he worked refitting ships, tearing out asbestos insulation. He also may have been exposed to the material in brake shoes, in his racing suit, or on sound stages (where it was also used as insulation.)

American specialists told him it was incurable. McQueen traveled to Mexico for laetrile treatments and coffee enemas, administered at a cost of $40,000 per month by a guy named William Donald Kelley. (Kelley was an ex-pat American, and an ex-dentist who wasn't even licensed to practice dentistry in the U.S. at that point.)

The story of McQueen's terminal cancer broke in National Enquirer. Kelley claimed that, any day, McQueen would be in complete remission and back at work. But instead, the cancer metastasized, forming massive tumors on his liver and neck. Once again, American surgeons refused to operate, because there was no chance he'd survive the surgery. McQueen returned to Mexico, checking into a clinic as 'Sam Sheperd'. He died in surgery.

Day 107 – **Ekins' career continued**

Ekins would've had a successful career either way, but his relationship with McQueen helped to cement his status as the top stunt man in Hollywood, for both car and cycle gigs.

Unlike Steve, he was gregarious and generous. When top European motocrossers started coming to the U.S. in the late '60s, Ekins' place was a home-away-from home.

Ekins worked into his sixties, devoting more and more time to his collection of 150 or so vintage bikes. He died in 2007, at the age of 77.

"I have heard people say that Bud was Steve McQueen's stuntman," Peter Starr wrote by way of obituary. "I like to think that Steve was Bud's actor. Ekins was the real thing."

Day 108 – **Another from Steve's small circle of friends burns out**

Kenny Howard's nom de plume, Von Dutch, was a reference to the Nazi imagery that inspired some of his work. Howard was a track star in high school, and had been known as "the fastest man in L.A."

He traveled in fast circles for a while; he was known in hot rodders as the best freehand pinstriper in SoCal. But as he got older, he became an eccentric near-hermit, living in a bus he'd converted into a camper/machine shop. He died in 1992, of complications related to booze.

Howard would've sneered at the fashion-world success of the 'Von Dutch' brand, which rose to prominence a decade after the real Von Dutch's death. The imagery currently associated with the brand is largely the work of a French fashion designer named Christian Audigier.

•

Day 109 – **A web site worth knowing: BikeEXIF**

www.bikeexif.com was one of the first web sites built around the idea of presenting slick pics of cool custom bikes – basically, it's Pornhub for gearheads.

Bike EXIF was one of the first web sites to present slick pics of cool custom bikes. It's basically Pornhub for gearheads, and the first port of call for custom builders to get exposure for their creations.

The site was started in 2008 by an ex-pat Englishman, Chris Hunter. Hunter used to be an advertising creative director, but when Bike EXIF started pulling in enough traffic to get noticed by advertisers, he quit his day job. These days, he lives on a farm in rural New Zealand and spends his time mending fences and battling a flaky internet connection.

People love to hate the hipster-custom culture that Hunter presents. But we have it on good authority that he thinks selvedge jeans look silly, has stubble on his chin rather than a full beard, and hates exhaust wrap with a passion. The truth is that in the last few years, Bike EXIF has become one of the most influential arbiters of motorcycle taste.

•

Other stars who really ride

It seems that Hollywood PR agents have a box to tick on their monthly worksheets, that says, "Make sure star is seen on motorcycle". Leave it to the paparazzi to publicize that trip to the manicurist.

Is there anything more eye-roll-inducing than Justin Bieber —wearing red sneakers and *sans* gloves—riding through Hollywood on a Ducati 848 with two-inch chicken strips? Ducati probably gave him that bike. Little did they realize that seeing an idiot like Bieber on a Ducati makes the brand less, not more, attractive.

Further along the spectrum towards legitimacy, there's guys like Ewan *'Long Way Round'* McGregor and David Beckham. Beckham and a few of his mates famously rode through the Amazonian back-roads, on Triumphs. Of course, the reason we know about McGregor and Beckham's 'adventure' rides is because they were followed by camera crews (and support trucks.)

If the thought of stars who only ride if there are cameras around to record them infuriates you, here is a list of celebrities who genuinely love bikes and ride to get away from cameras, not to attract them...

Day 110 – **Leno's garage is his sanctuary**

Jay Leno is perhaps the best-known car- and bike-nut in television. His 'garage'—a complex of several large buildings near the Burbank airport—holds hundreds of vintage cars and bikes. Leno makes a point of riding (and driving) every one of them at least once a year. Regulars at the Rock Store café, in the mountains above Malibu, see him there all the time.

Although Jay keeps a staff of several mechanics and restorers employed full-time, he still loves to get his hands dirty, too.

The Leno collection's worth millions, which begs the question of what will happen to it when Jay finally auditions his standup act for Saint Peter (not that I expect that to happen any time soon!)

Day 111 – **Lyle's favorite kind'a country: cross-country**

Lyle Lovett may not be the biggest country music star—in fact he may be better known as Julia Roberts' ex-husband than he is as a singer—but he's certainly one of the most avid riders on this list.

Lovett started riding as a kid, and raced motocross in high school. His first job was at Cycle Shack, a Penton dealership in Houston. Years later, he owned Houston dealership, but he's since sold it. (As befits a country musician, he rides horses, too.)

Lovett was inspired to write his song *'The Road to Ensenada'* after breaking his collarbone on an adventurous ride down the Baja Peninsula. I'm not sure what he rides on the street these days, but for years he rode a Ducati 916 and then a Ducati 998R through the Texas hill country.

Day 112 – **Keanu Reeves builds a ~~neo~~ new bike**

Keanu Reeves is a famously impassive actor, but he's genuinely passionate about motorcycles—to the point where he may now be better-known as a bike builder than actor.

According to Reeves, he's only ever owned two cars and prefers to use two wheels almost exclusively for transportation. For years he was seen on vintage Nortons, though he's owned and ridden everything from Kawasaki enduros to a GSX-R750, to a Harley Shovelhead.

Reeves and a business partner, Gard Hollinger, have formed a company called Arch Motorcycles, and released their first model, the KRGT-1. It's a muscle cruiser powered by a 102 cu. in. S&S v-twin.

The KRGT-1 has two fuel cells, which are machined from solid, beginning life as a 534-pound aluminum billet. That's a lotta' swarf. It's also a lotta' dough. MSRP was initially set at $78,000.

Day 113 – **Hugh loves bikes**

British actor and comedian Hugh Laurie has enjoyed a remarkably varied career but he's best known to American audiences as 'House', the crabby, brilliant doctor character he plays on that TV show.

Laurie's ridden his entire life. He even convinced the producers of *House* to write motorcycling into his character. The doctor, who limps and pops pain pills, still manages to arrive at work on a Honda CBR, with his cane strapped on as luggage.

Although they explain the limp in the show—an infarction in the thigh muscle that caused him to have dead tissue amputated—I don't think they ever tell viewers how that injury occurred. Maybe it was a motorcycle accident.

Day 114 – **Like you, Daniel Day-Lewis shifts gears with his left foot**

Daniel Day-Lewis—or should we be correct and refer to him as Sir Daniel? —is one of the most highly-regarded actors of all time. He's utterly devoted to his craft, to the point of remaining in character for the entire duration of every film shoot. It must work for him, because he's the only man who's ever won the 'Best Actor' Oscar three times: for *'Lincoln'*, *'There Will Be Blood'*, and *'My Left Foot'*.

When he's not making movies, he still lives in Northern Ireland, where he rides motorcycles all the time. He admits to being a Valentino Rossi groupie, and is is fast friends with real-roads legend Phillip McCallen; he's occasionally seen at Phil's shop in Lisburn, or at Irish meetings like the epic NW200.

Day 115 – **Pink**

Brad Pitt and Angelina Jolie have been spotted riding motorcycles together, but a cele-biking couple with motor oil in their veins are FMX star Carey Hart and his pop-star wife Pink.

Alicia Beth 'Pink' Moore proposed to Hart by holding out a pit board reading "Will You Marry Me?" at a motorcycle event. She's released a few posed publicity shots on motorcycles that probably aren't hers, which causes me to mark her down a bit on the cred-meter, but she's been seen out and about on her own cruisers. When her parenting skills were questioned after pictures surfaced of Hart riding his motocross bike with their two-year-old daughter Willow perched on the tank, she fiercely defended herself on social media.

Day 116 – **The *Lincoln Lawyer* would rather ride**

Matthew McConaughey rode a Triumph in *'How to Lose a Guy in 10 Days'*, but he's owned a bunch of bikes. One that he sold off was a chopper commemorating the Texas Longhorns' national championship win. The proceeds of that sale went to the Texas Exes Scholarship Fund and the actor's own Just Keep Livin' Foundation.

Day 117 – That's not a huge phallic symbol he's riding, that's his...

Motorcycle haters often characterize bikes as phallic symbols and suggest that we ride them to make up for certain, um, deficiencies. That's presumably not Michael Fassbender's motivation.

A few years ago, the actor got his (ahem) seminal role in 'Shame', which included some on-screen full-frontal nudity. His co-star Charlize Theron joked, "[Fassbender's] penis was a revelation. I'm available to work with it any time!"

But seriously, folks... Fassbender was terrific in the role and some people were surprised he didn't win more awards for it. There was even speculation that the males who vote on such things ignored him because they were jealous (and not of his motorcycles.)

Before Fassbender got that big role, he starred in a short called 'Man on a Motorcycle' about a day in the life of a London bike courier. He has high-mileage days of his own; he recently took off on a multi-thousand-mile motorcycle road trip between films, and sometimes still rides with his dad, who is also a bike nut.

Day 118 – Honda gave John Travolta an early boost

John Travolta is seen on motorcycles from time to time, which isn't really enough to warrant being included on this list I suppose. But he gets a special place here because long before he was a star, he appeared riding a Honda motorcycle in some of the famous "You meet the nicest people on a Honda" TV commercials.

His co-star in one of those spots was none other than Malcolm Smith. The commercials are worth searching for on YouTube.

Day 119 – **The Diavel made him do it**

Bradley Cooper's gravitated to films with motorcycle themes, such as *The Place Beyond the Pines* and films he get to ride in, like *Burnt*. In that movie, he plays a bad-boy chef who rides a Ducati Diavel.

Not long after it was filmed, life imitated art when Cooper went out on a date with Lady Gaga… on his Diavel.

Day 120 – **The Boss can be hard core**

Bruce Springsteen once showed up at Billy Joel's 20th Century Cycles shop and insisted on taking the piano man's bobber for a ride, despite the fact that temperatures were well below freezing. He returned so enthusiastic about the bike that he immediately commissioned 20th Century to make one for him.

Springsteen's bike was built up using a modern 'retro' motor—sourced from the under-appreciated Kawasaki W650 (sadly no longer imported into the U.S.)

Day 121 – **Tommy Lee**

Tommy Lee learned to ride from his pal, ex-AMA motocross and supermoto champion Micky Dymond. In hindsight, it's possible that Tommy Lee should *not* have learned from someone who spent most of his time on two wheels either sliding sideways or flying through the air.

Tommy Lee once had a massive wipe-out on the freeway in L.A. To make matters worse, he was giving 'Armored Saint' bassist Joey Vera a ride. Lee escaped with minor injuries, but Vera's hand was mangled, and he couldn't play his bass for months. (I guess he wasn't a sufficiently armored saint.)

Lee was not discouraged. In fact, he continues to sponsor an annual charity motorcycle 'run', in Pittsburg, Texas.

Day 122 – **Jamie Oliver and Mario Batali**

Several real-life celebrity chefs ride, but since the life of a chef is all about shopping for ingredients and scouring crowded farmer's markets, they tend to use scooters around town.

Jamie Oliver used to be seen riding around London on a Vespa, and Mario Batali uses one to slip though New York City's gridlock. Mario's apparently hooked on transcendental meditation, and once told Bon Appetit magazine that he meditated while riding his scooter down Ninth Avenue.

Batali's got his own signature line of Orange Crocs, but if he's going to zone out in Manhattan traffic, he should probably consider a more ATTGATT approach

Day 123 – **A prince…**

Prince William, Duke of Cambridge, aka Catherine Middleton's husband, aka future Kind of England, is an avid motorcyclist, who rides a Ducati 1198 S Corse on the street—that must drive his protection detail batty. He also keeps dirt bikes on various family estates. His little brother Harry rides too, and the two of them once led a 5,000-mile motorcycle trip across Africa in support of the Tusk Trust, a wildlife conservation group.

You can love or hate the idea of a Royal Family, but William's a man's man who has a day job (and often, a night job) flying an air ambulance helicopter.

Day 124 – ...and, 'Prince'

Prince's bike was a 1981 Honda CM400 'Hondamatic'. (Trust Prince to choose a bike notable for its tranny.) From an engineering perspective, the Hondamatic is kind of cool. There's a fluidic primary drive (between the crankshaft and transmission) that allows the user to bring the bike to a stop, in gear, without stalling or pulling in a clutch. It doesn't even have a clutch; that lever on the left handlebar is actually a parking brake. The user can shift gears just by rolling off the throttle and nudging a shift lever. It's equipped with a simple two-speed tranny.

On the face of it, creating a full sized motorcycle that was easy to operate seemed like a good idea. Honda made sure it had a low seat height, so it would be beginner friendly in other ways, too. That might have been what attracted the 5'2" singer to the model. Still, it was a commercial flop. Honda made versions of the little bike from 1978-'83.

I suppose it might have caught on if they'd kept it in the line-up another year, because *Purple Rain* came out in 1984. As if Prince's CM400 wasn't homely enough, he put a massive Vetter Windjammer fairing on his. The bike was purple—duh! —in Purple Rain and then resprayed black and gold for *Graffiti Bridge* in 1990.

Day 125 – **A shout-out to a country legend**

One celeb who might not be an avid rider herself—but who has been a great friend to the sport of motorcycling—is country music legend Loretta Lynn.

Loretta owns a sprawling ranch 65 miles west of Nashville, in Hurricane Mills, TN. It's just north of Bucksnort, TN (a name that I couldn't have made up.)

Once a year, the place is given over to youth/amateur motocross; it's the site of the AMA's amateur championship, drawing thousands of racers in dozens of age categories and classes. Since 1982, winning at "Loretta Lynn's" has pretty much been the last step before turning pro for every American motocross or supercross star.

Her commitment to the sport is especially noteworthy because the rest of the year, Loretta Lynn's is devoted to horses. There's not really even a permanent track on the property. The fact that it's not used year 'round was actually part of Dave Coombs' vision for an AMA amateur championship race. That way, no one would have a home-track advantage.

Day 126 – **Buddy Holly**

In 1958, Buddy Holly and two members of his band The Crickets were already big stars, but when they arrived at a Dallas Harley-Davidson dealership to buy bikes, the salesman didn't recognize them, and told them not to touch the motorcycles!

Holly and his pals then hit Ray Miller Triumph, where they each picked a bike; he chose an Ariel Cyclone.

After Holly was killed in a plane crash, his dad kept the Ariel for a long time. It eventually changed hands a couple of times, until two surviving members of The Crickets re-acquired it and gave it to Waylon Jennings, who had been a good friend of Buddy Holly.

The motorcycle is now on display at the Buddy Holly Center in Lubbock, Texas.

•

Day 127 – A web site worth knowing: Pipeburn

www.pipeburn.com is another antipodean site devoted to a curated selection of customized and restored motorcycles. It's produced by two guys named Scott Hopkin and Andrew Jones. If you can't get enough fiberglass-tape-wrapped headers or huge block-tread tires on street bikes, Pipeburn will happily provide a daily fix.

Pipeburn's slick art direction and high-end photography illustrate the fact that – as is the case with BikeEXIF – the proprietors of this site came up in the ad business.

•

The days the music died (or almost)

What is it with musicians and motorcycles?!?

Day 128 – Even *portraying* a musician is dangerous

Gary Busey, the actor who portrayed Buddy in *The Buddy Holly Story* almost died in a motorcycle crash.

Ironically, Busey had been a vocal opponent of mandatory helmet laws. In 1988, he picked up his motorcycle at Bartel's Harley Davidson and only got a block and a half before running wide around a corner and hitting a curb. With his bare head.

Had he been wearing a helmet, he would have walked away. As it was, Busey claims he had a near-death experience. It couldn't have been too terrifying because after he finally recovered he *still* argued against helmet laws.

That's more proof that the expression, "knock some sense into him" is, itself, almost always nonsense. But if you want a real argument in favor of helmets, consider this: Before hitting his noggin, Busey was nominated for an Academy Award for his role as Buddy Holly and had roles in critically acclaimed and cult movies like *Straight Time* and *Big Wednesday*. After his brain injury, he starred in *Celebrity Rehab with Dr. Drew*.

Day 129 – The Piano Man almost became the 'no-piano' man

Billy Joel may be the pop star who is most committed to motorcycling. He has a shop that sells and customizes bikes—20th Century Cycles—in a town known as Oyster

Bay, Long Island. Joel's take on the custom scene often involves taking modern 'retro' bikes like Hinckley Triumphs and customizing them to make them look more authentic, while maintaining modern ease-of-use.

In 1982, Joel T-boned a car driven by a woman who ran a red light directly in his path. His left thumb was crushed, and his right wrist was dislocated.

"I was never worried whether I'd play again," Joel told Mike Seate, "I was never that good to begin with."

He won a slew of Grammys after the crash, which didn't discourage him from riding. He usually has about 40 bikes in his personal stable. His shop is also a destination for a popular Long Island "bike night" on Tuesdays all summer long.

Day 130 – **A Buckaroo gets bucked off**

Donald Eugene Ulrich was better known as 'Don Rich', an influential country musician who helped define the genre's 'Bakersfield Sound' in the 1960s. He played fiddle and guitar, and was a member of Buck Owens' Buckaroos.

Even if you're not a country fan, you'd recognize the hook from their 1963 hit, *Act Naturally*. That was a song that Don convinced Buck to record, and the first song on which Don played lead guitar.

A few years later, Rich was a key member of the Buckaroos when they recorded a live album at Carnegie Hall. It's considered to be one of the best live country albums of all time.

Buck Owens always worried when Don rode his motorcycle. In 1974, Don left a recording session at Buck's Bakersfield studio, heading for a family vacation on the central coast. Don crashed, inexplicably, hitting a median in the middle of Highway 1 in Morro Bay. There were no skid marks and no indication of mechanical failure.

Buck Owens could not bring himself to talk about the death of his friend for years. But eventually he said, "I think my music life ended when he died. Oh yeah, I carried on and I existed, but the real joy and love, the real lightning and thunder is gone forever."

Day 131 – **Lucker runs out**

Before I started writing this book, I didn't even know there was a style of music called 'deathcore'. Nor did I know there was a band called 'Suicide Silence'. But, those are real things. Or at least they were until Mitch Lucker, the lead singer for Suicide Silence, lost control of his Harley-Davidson on the evening of Halloween, 2012.

Lucker then performed a high-speed slam dance picking a Huntington Beach light pole as a partner. His motorcycle continued on for few yards before slamming into a pickup truck. Luckily neither the occupants of the truck nor nearby trick-or-treaters were injured.

Suicide Silence's second album was called *No Time To Bleed*.

Day 132 – **Is that a *Rebel Yell*, or are you just screaming?**

In 1990, Billy Idol ran a stop sign in L.A., which wouldn't have been a problem except there was a car in the intersection. He suffered a severely broken leg, and for a time there was doubt that surgeons could even save the limb.

"I didn't give a fuck really," said the singer —whose real name is Michael Albert Broad. "Because when you're dosed out of your mind on morphine, the world is quite a pleasant place. It's coming off morphine that's the real bastard. You're lying there with a smashed leg and you've got cold turkey. That was really heavy."

The injury didn't just mess up the rock singer's performance schedule, it cost him a great acting job. Idol had been director James Cameron's pick to play the villainous T-1000 robot in *Terminator 2*. Idol's first wreck wasn't enough to stop him from riding though. Years later, he suffered a hairline fracture when he ran into a truck tire that was lying in the road.

Day 133 – **Oh man, not again!**

Duane Allman was ranked by Guitar Player magazine as one of the greatest rock players of his generation. He's best known as the leader of the Allman Brothers band, though he was also a terrific session man, who worked with Eric Clapton, Aretha Franklin, and Wilson Pickett.

In 1971, his band was riding high on the success of their live album *'At Fillmore East'*. Allman was taking time off in his home town of Macon.

He unwound by riding his Harley Sportster, but while he was a master of the slide guitar, he was less skilled at sliding motorcycles.

A lumber truck slowed unexpectedly as it crossed an intersection ahead of him, and Allman lost control as he swerved to avoid it. He hit the truck or, by some (even more horrific) accounts, the heavy metal ball dangling off the truck's crane. He was traveling at a high enough speed that he was found 90' from the truck he hit. 'Skydog' was alive at the hospital, but died hours later as a result of massive internal injuries.

Tragically, Allman Brothers bassist Berry Oakley died in a motorcycle crash just a few blocks away, almost exactly a year after his friend.

Day 134 – **Music's most mysterious motorcycle mishap**

Bob Dylan loved motorcycles, and bought a new Triumph T100 Tiger when he moved into New York City in his early 20s. Back then, Joan Baez was a frequently terrified passenger.

Luckily, he didn't have any passengers on July 29, 1966, when he crashed on the outskirts of Woodstock, NY. He left his manager's house in the nearby community of West Saugherties, trailed by his new wife, who was driving a car. Dylan himself gave different accounts of the crash; he hit oil, he was blinded by the sun. He later said that he broke vertebrae.

Whatever the extent of those injuries, he canceled upcoming performances. Dylan toured and performed constantly in the five years before the crash, but —

although he recorded over 100 songs — he performed in public only a handful of times in the eight years that followed the incident.

This story is shrouded in mystery. There were rumors that the entire incident was just a cover, and that Dylan was really out of the public eye because he was doing a stretch in rehab.

It's science, but it works like magic

The basic principles by which internal combustion engines work are pretty simple—it comes down to 'suck-squeeze-bang-blow', as they say. We already know the names of quite a few of the engineers, designers, and early mechanics who perfected the motorcycle.

Guys like Daimler or deDion were clever engineers; they filed patents and in some cases made fortunes. But they would never have done those things if they hadn't been preceded by the physicists, chemists, and mathematicians who discovered the basic scientific principles *behind* sucking, squeezing, banging, and blowing. Here's a list of guys who pursued that knowledge for its own sake. They didn't even live to see a world of cars and motorcycles, but their ideas shaped virtually every modern vehicle.

Fair warning: Looking out at 21st century America—especially in election years—it's depressing to realize that stupid is the new smart. So maybe you *shouldn't* drop these names at your local bike night.

Day 135 – **Antoine-Laurent de Lavoisier
(France, 1743-'94)**

You can't grok internal combustion until you grok
combustion. Lavoisier was the first person to accurately
describe what was happening when things burned and
released energy. Until he came along, people had all kinds
of theories, usually involving some mysterious property or
invisible material called 'phlogiston'.

In 1772, Lavoisier carefully weighed the products of
burned sulfur and realized that the resultant ash was
heavier than the sulfur he'd begun with. He postulated that
there was a component of the atmosphere that combined
with sulfur during combustion.

At around the same time, the English chemist Joseph
Priestly and a Swede, Carl Wilhelm Scheele, were also
studying a component of the atmosphere that seemed to be
essential to combustion. Priestley heated the metallic ash
of mercury and found it released a gas which was identical
to one that Scheele determined had to be present for
combustion to occur. Lavoisier called that gas 'oxygen'.

Lavoisier obviously had a good head on his shoulders…
for a while. He was a hated member of the aristocracy, and
was guillotined during the French Revolution.

Day 136 – **Sadi Carnot (France 1796-1832)**

Carnot was a physicist and engineer. He lived at a time
when the first steam engines had already been
demonstrated, although scientists could not yet explain
how they worked. Carnot was the first guy who really

understood the way heat energy was being converted into mechanical work.

He wrote *'Reflections on the Motive Power of Fire'* when he was just 28. His theory was not immediately appreciated. He died of cholera at the age of 36. No one understood the exact nature of that disease at the time; out of fear, most of his possessions and writings were buried with him!

Steam engines can produce massive power, but their specific horsepower (the ratio of power to displacement) is less than gasoline engines. That's why very, very early in the evolution of the motorcycle, inventors gave up on steam power. Rudolf Diesel credited Carnot for inspiring his work on internal combustion engines.

Day 137 – **Rudolph Clausius (Poland, 1822-'88)**

Clausius was a Pomeranian. No, not a tiny yapping dog, but rather a person from Pomerania — which was a German principality in his day (and is now part of Poland.)

He was the father of the kinetic theory of gases. In 1850, he published a paper entitled, *On The Moving Force of Heat*, in which he outlined some key scientific principles that, in coming decades, were put to work in internal combustion engines.

His wife, Adelheid, died in childbirth in 1875, leaving him to raise their six kids alone. He continued to teach, but found that he had little time for research. Luckily by then, he'd already advanced the science that would be applied by future engineers.

Along with Carnot, he helped to define the Second Law of Thermodynamics which can be used to determine the efficiency of any internal combustion engine.

Day 138 – **Robert William Boyle (Anglo-Irish, 1627-'91)**

Boyle, who was born in Ireland, is considered to be the father of modern chemistry and the scientific method.

He was one of 14 children, and was handed off into foster care at a young age. He spoke English, Irish, Latin, and Greek by the time he was eight. He seems to have always been a scientist, and once wrote out a list of 24 things he'd like to invent. One entry on that list was, "potent drugs to alter or exalt imagination, waking, memory and other functions and appease pain, procure innocent sleep, harmless dreams, etc."

While he didn't invent LSD, his scientific study of air pumps laid the groundwork for all future piston engines. He's best known for Boyle's Law, which basically explains why a piston compresses your air-fuel mixture, and why the pressure in your combustion chamber drives that piston back down.

Day 139 – **Daniel Bernoulli (Holland, 1700-'82)**

Bernoulli was a Dutchman who lived in Switzerland. He was the son of an almost-equally famous mathematician, Johann Bernoulli. When he and his dad tied for first place in science contest sponsored by the University of Paris, his father disowned him.

Bernoulli (the whippersnapper) is now remembered for Bernoulli's Principle, which states that an increase in the speed of a fluid occurs simultaneously with a decrease in pressure. Bernoulli did the basic science that, in later years, would underlie all carburetors and fuel injection systems. His principle, for example, explains why air rushing through a carburetor will suck gasoline up through a carb jet.

Speaking of gasoline, I suppose an honorable mention should go to an American, William Merriam Burton. He was the chemist who patented thermal cracking, which doubled the amount of gasoline that could be extracted from crude oil. He became the President of Standard Oil from 1918-'27.

Day 140 – **Alessandro Volta (Italy, 1745-1827)**

Volta lived on the beautiful shores of Lake Como, in Italy. He leant his name to 'volt', which gives you some idea of the importance of his early research into electricity.

Volta and another Italian, Luigi Galvani, experimented with what they at first called 'animal electricity'. They connected a frog's leg with two metals in series, and saw the frog's leg convulse. Volta and Galvani argued about the exact nature of what they were seeing. Volta realized that the frog's leg was a conductor, not the source of the energy they were seeing.

To settle that argument, Volta invented the first battery, proving that it was the metals (in that case, zinc and copper) and not the frog's leg, that generated the current.

So if you are one of the motorcyclists who would rather push a starter button than kick it over, you can thank Alessandro Volta. He also was the first person to ignite methane by using a spark in a closed container.

Day 141 – **Michael Faraday (England, 1791-1867)**

Magnetos, generators, and starter motors all go back to the fundamental research of Michael Faraday, an Englishman who lived south of London.

Although his influence on the modern motorcycle began when he invented the dynamo in 1831, Faraday's research in both chemistry and the field of electro-magnetics went way beyond that. Einstein kept a portrait of Faraday in his office for inspiration.

Despite Faraday's obvious genius, he was not considered a 'gentleman' by the English aristocracy. Perhaps because he felt looked down upon, he once rejected an honorary doctorate, believing that it was contrary to the word of the Bible to collect earthly rewards or riches. During the Crimean War, the British government asked for his advice on the production of chemical weapons and he again refused on ethical grounds.

Day 142 – **Heinrich Ruhmkorff (Germany, 1803-'77)**

Faraday's work paved the way for a variety of low-voltage apparatuses, but when it came to providing a high voltage spark for early internal combustion engines, someone had to invent the induction coil. The guy who's credited with perfecting it is Ruhmkorff, a German who worked in England and then settled in Paris.

An Englishman, Nicholas Callan, demonstrated the first coil in 1836. Ruhmkorff then took turns with an American, E.S. Ritchie, in improving the design.

Ruhmkorff's device generated enough voltage to send a spark a foot through the air. He was assigned a key patent on the invention in 1851, and he was awarded a 50,000-franc prize by Napoleon III, who called it the most important discovery in the application of electricity.

Whether it was really the single most important discovery in the field or not, it was definitely a spark of genius. So, I'm putting in a plug for him, by including him on this list.

Day 143 – **Ismail al-Jazari (Turkey, 1136-1206)**

So, by now we've got pistons moving up and down, but how about converting that reciprocating motion into rotation? The first guy to describe a connecting rod and crankshaft apparatus was Ismail al-Jazari.

al-Jazari was a Muslim scholar and engineer who lived in what is now Turkey. In his time, Arabic scholars were the world's most sophisticated mathematicians. But as clever as al-Jasazi was, he seems to have perfected his machines by trial and error rather than calculation.

His con-rod and crankshaft invention is described in his *Book of Knowledge of Ingenious Mechanical Devices*, where it is applied in a two-cylinder water pump. That was one of about 100 devices described in the book, which was a best-seller in the days before printing presses, when each copy had to be written and illustrated by scribes. (I wonder if he invented any machines to treat writer's cramp?)

As if that wasn't a big enough contribution to mechanics, al-Jazari also invented the camshaft, which he used in some ingenious time-keeping devices.

Day 144 – **Hero of Alexandria (Egypt, c10-70 AD)**

Transmitting the power of a spinning crankshaft to your wheels takes… gears.

The first description of transmission of power with gears is attributed to Hero of Alexandria, who is also credited with inventing the first windmill, a primitive steam engine known as the 'Hero Engine', and (I'm not making this up) the first vending machine.

Many of Hero's inventions were devices used in Greek theater or in temples, where they may well have helped priests to convince their followers that they were capable of magic.

Day 145 – **Blaise Pascal (France, 1623-'62)**

Pascal is now remembered more for his contributions to pure math and philosophy, but he made an important contribution to your personal safety.

When you think about it, your motorcycle's front brake is by far the most powerful component on your bike. (The proof of that statement is that you can *decelerate* from 100 miles per hour in less time and distance, using your brake, than it took you to *reach* 100 mph using the motor. Are you still with me?)

So how does your right hand generate that much power? The answer is: Pascal's Law: pressure exerted anywhere in a confined incompressible fluid is transmitted equally in all directions throughout the fluid such that the pressure variations (initial differences) remain the same.

Thanks to Pascal's Law, you can use your brake lever to exert a large force across a tiny surface area in your brake's master cylinder, and have that same force applied across the much larger surface area of your brake pads.

So a Frenchman who died 350 years ago has literally saved your ass, many times. Cool fact: He was born in Clermont-Ferrand, Michelin's home town.

Day 146 – **Jacques Charles (France, 1746-1823)**

Charles was (yet another!) Frenchman, who was famous in his day for conceiving, making, and testing the first hydrogen balloon. Charles demonstrated his lighter-than-air vehicle for the first time in Paris, on the Champ de Mars—that's where the Eiffel Tower stands now. Benjamin Franklin was in the crowd, watching. The balloon flew for 45 minutes, pursued by spectators on horseback. It landed in a field north of Paris where terrified peasants destroyed it with pitchforks and scythes.

What does any of that have to do with you? Two things: First, if you're going to crash, try to avoid a field full of furious peasants. And second, his discoveries govern many aspects of the way both motors and tires work.

If you're a serious motorcyclist, you set cold tire pressures lower than the optimum operating pressure for the tire, because as acceleration and braking forces heat your tire carcass, the pressure inside the tire will rise. Not only that, starting out 'too soft' will actually make it easier for you to get your tire up to proper working temperature.

Next time someone asks you why that is, tell them: Charles's Law.

Cool fact: The first person to accurately describe the way gases expand when heated was Joseph Louis Lussac, in 1802. But as a true gentleman, Lussac dubbed his theory 'Charles's Law' because he admitted that while he was the first to *publish* the law, Jacques Charles *discovered* it.

Deal Breakers

Over the years, much has been made of the engineers and entrepreneurs who created great motorcycles and great motorcycle companies. But what about the people – or circumstances – that killed companies or hurt motorcycling? Herewith, a brief survey of failures, flops, and fiascos...

Day 147 – **Rodney C. Gott**

Most Harley-Davidson fans agree that the low point in the company's long history came in the 1970s – when the company was owned by American Machine & Foundry. Those 'AMF' years are remembered as a time of falling quality and low investment in R&D, while the quality of Japanese imports (especially) was on the rise.

It might be an oversimplification to blame the AMF 'merger' for all Harley's problems in that decade. Were it not for AMF's financial wherewithal, the company may not have survived at all.

But it's true that AMF strained relationships with Union workers, refused to invest in the tooling required to produce a modern motorcycle that could compete with increasingly sophisticated imports, and put sales ahead of quality control, to say the least. If you're going to blame one guy for that, blame AMF Chairman and CEO Rodney C. Gott.

Gott was a West Point graduate and a certified WWII hero. He was also a motorcyclist who knew what he was getting into. It should've been a good fit, but Gott ran AMF the way he'd commanded XII Corps Field Artillery. He gave orders and it was up to his managers to hit their targets. In 1971, H-D made 16,000 Big Twins; in '76 it made 48,000. At the end of every month, factories raced pell mell to make their numbers. Frustrated workers sometimes actively sabotaged bikes on the production line.

Gott retired right at the end of the decade, and AMF came under the control of a new boss, Tom York, who was an accountant with no particular love for motorcycles. At that point, in order to save the brand, Vaughn Beals suggested that AMF divest itself of Harley-Davidson. And the rest is history...

Day 148 – **Import Tariffs**

If you prowl Craigslist looking for mid- '80s superbikes, you may be baffled to see ads for 700cc Honda Interceptors, and Yamaha FZ700s. "Weren't those supposed to be 750cc models?" you might wonder.

They were 750s in the rest of the world. But those fabulous bikes were sleeved down in the U.S. because in the early '80s, Harley-Davidson petitioned the U.S. International Trade Commission – asking the ITC to impose import tariffs on motorcycles over 700cc.

Ronald Reagan didn't want to be known as the President who'd killed Harley-Davidson, so he signed the tariff into law in 1983 – against his instincts, and in spite of the fact that experts had testified that the tariffs would hurt American motorcyclists by raising prices and restricting the number of new models available to us.

At the time most of the biggest Japanese bikes were 750cc. Rather than add hundreds of dollars to the price of those models, Honda and Yamaha just sold 699cc versions here. (Although under the final terms of the tariff, they could, and did, import some 750 cc models, too.)

To its credit, the Reagan administration insisted that the industry be regularly reviewed, and that the tariff should come off at whatever point Harley-Davidson's survival was no longer under threat. And to Harley's credit, Vaughn Beals told the ITC that it could drop the tariff a year before the five-year term was due to expire.

Day 149 – **Can't-am Motorcycles**

Bombardier's Can-am brand broke cover at the 1973 ISDT. It became impossible to ignore in '74, when the MX-1 125cc motocross bike dominated its class in the AMA national championship. It was an auspicious start, to say the least. And, since Bombardier's Ski-Doo brand already had a network of thousands of dealers in place, things looked awfully good for Can-am. At the time, most of its competitors were relatively small European companies like Husqvarna.

Unfortunately, the brand came on the scene just as well-financed Japanese brands like Honda and Yamaha were turning their attention to motocross. They soon neutralized the advantage Can-am had with its powerful Rotax motors. Then, the Japs turned their attention to suspension and brakes – leaving Can-am in the dust, literally.

Bombardier couldn't justify the R&D cost of keeping up. Around 1980, the Canadians decided to abandon bikes and shift that effort into its new Sea-Doo line. The Can-am brand persisted for another few years, but the motorcycles were built by Armstrong/CCM, in England. The last Can-Ams were built in 1987.

Day 150 – **State Farm's insurance blacklist**

The mid-1980s was a Golden Age in terms of sportbike design. We saw the first GSX-R750 and the Honda RC30 arrive on the scene, then the GSX-R1100. Speed-obsessed bikers weren't the only ones that noticed a quantum jump in motorcycle speed and power. The Insurance Institute for Highway Safety released a safety 'study' in 1987 that openly recommended banning such "bullet bikes".

The next year, State Farm – the largest insurer of cars and motorcycles in the U.S. at the time – sent a 'blacklist' memo to all its agents, telling them not to issue policies on 38 models from the Honda CX500 Turbo to the Yamaha FJ1200.

Motorcyclists were understandably outraged. So were agents who realized that families with two cars and a motorcycle were inclined to shift all their policies to competing firms.

State Farm had probably hoped that other leading insurers would follow suit; when they didn't, State Farm issued as shorter list of just 29 bikes – and told agents there was some flexibility in the policy, in order to prevent losing good customers.

Faced with vocal criticism from the AMA, customer defections, and competitors who were using sport bike riders as 'foot in the door' for auto and home policies, State Farm had to admit it was fighting a losing battle. It officially killed the blacklist in February, '89.

Day 151 – No Brainers: Helmet Laws

The 1966 Highway Safety Act authorized the US secretary of transportation to withhold up to 10% of federal highway funds from states that did not mandate the use of crash helmets. That worked, and by 1975, 47 states and the District of Columbia had universal motorcycle helmet laws.

In 1976, states successfully lobbied Congress to stop the Department of Transportation from assessing financial penalties on states without helmet laws. Within a few years, dozens of states had repealed some or all of their helmet laws.

Congress tried to apply similar pressure to the states again in 1991, when the Intermodal Surface Transportation Efficiency Act offered grants to states that enacted helmet laws, and sanctions against those that didn't. That lasted until 1995 when the National Highway System Designation Act again left the matter up to the states.

Day 152 – Flightless Bird: Corbin Sparrow

In the 1990s, Mike Corbin (of motorcycle seat fame) created the Corbin Sparrow, a three-wheeled, fully-enclosed electric vehicle intended for short-range urban commutes.

The Sparrow is literally laughable now; that's why villains use them to chase Austin Powers in 'Goldmember'. But it was a hit when it was unveiled at the 1996 San Francisco Auto Show. In those days of the first dot-com boom, Corbin took thousands of deposits.

That left him with the challenge of delivering vehicles. He made a few hundred of them before declaring bankruptcy in 2003 – the victim of supplier issues, the dot-com bust, and the range limitations of the Sparrow's crude lead-acid batteries.

Day 153 – **CPSC Trike Ban**

Honda introduced its first balloon-tired 'All-Terrain Cycle', the ATC90, in 1970. It was an immediate hit, and Honda continued to develop three-wheelers well into the 1980s, when it shifted emphasis to four-wheeled models.

Although those first Honda trikes weren't fast, they quickly began accounting for an alarming number of injuries (230,000) and even deaths (644). About half those casualties were children, and by the mid- '80s the American Academy of Pediatricians called for a moratorium on ATV sales.

While it was certainly possible to use a Honda ATC safely, they *were* pretty unstable. Honda settled lawsuits filed by parents who claimed that Honda's advertising led them to believe the trikes were suitable for use by kids.

The Consumer Product Safety Commission served notice on the ATV industry in 1985 that it would regulate three-wheelers. At the end of '87, Honda and four other companies signed Consent Decrees effectively banning the trikes. While the Consent Decrees have since lapsed (and in spite of the fact that Honda's 'Big Red' trike had plenty of fans, mainly hunters and others who loved its all-terrain capability) the trikes have never really reappeared in the marketplace.

Day 154 – **Dennis Poore**

No one person can be blamed for killing the British motorcycle industry, but the final coup de grace was administered by Roger Dennistoun 'Dennis' Poore.

Poore was a rich racing driver in the 1950s. He became chairman of Manganese Bronze Holdings, a company that previously manufactured boat propellers. Beginning in the '60s, he acquired a bunch of failing British motorcycle brands, including Norton and Matchless, which became subsidiaries of Manganese Bronze.

By 1972, Triumph had merged with BSA and BSA/Triumph merged with Manganese Bronze's motorcycle holdings to create a new company, Norton Villiers Triumph. Poore was the Chairman of that company, and for a while there was real hope that he could salvage at least one British motorcycle company.

However, his strategy involved cutting thousands of jobs. When Triumph workers got wind of his plans, they locked management out of Triumph's factory in Meriden. The "workers' co-op" actually outlasted NVT, and continued to make Triumphs until 1983. They characterized Poore, to the end, as an asset-stripper.

In Poore's defense, it's possible that if the workers had agreed to work with him, Triumph might never have shut down. Whether you blame him or not, he was the man at the controls of the British motorcycle industry when it crashed.

Day 155 – **Honda tires of competition: Bridgestone**

The Bridgestone company was founded in the 1930s by Shojiro Ishibashi. The company name is a play on the founder's name ('ishi' = stone, 'bashi' = bridge). Although it began as a textile business, it soon settled on making tires.

After WWII, Bridgestone made bicycles, and later bicycles equipped with small clip-on motors. By the late 1950s, Bridgestone was making small motorcycles. Bridgestone survived a period of consolidation in the Japanese motorcycle industry in the early 1960s; in fact, it benefitted from the failure of Lilac and Tohatsu because it recruited their engineers. For a time in the mid- '60s, Bridgestone's disc-valve two-strokes, such as the 350cc GTR twin, were among the fastest Japanese production bikes.

However, production had ceased by the end of the decade. Officially, Bridgestone's story was that the company needed to expand tire production and there was simply no room in the factory for the less-profitable motorcycle lines.

Unofficially, the other big Japanese manufacturers – notably Honda – told Bridgestone that if it wanted to continue supplying them with tires, it'd better stop competing with them in the motorcycle market.

Day 156 – **Indian's WWI strategic error**

Both Harley-Davidson and Indian supplied the U.S. Army with motorcycles during the First World War, though Harley sold about 20,000 bikes to Indian's 50,000. Harley-Davidson could have filled more orders from the Army, but it was careful to keep its U.S. dealer network well supplied with civilian bikes.

By contrast, Indian was happy to sell almost all the bikes it could make to the Government. Doing so allowed the Wigwam – which was already cash-strapped in 1917 – to save on advertising and warranty costs.

The problem was that doing that starved Indian dealers of new bikes. Many of them abandoned Indian and became Harley dealers. Although Indian limped along for decades, it never fully recovered.

Day 157 – **Paris bans old bikes**

Effective July 1, 2016 the city of Paris banned motorcycles older than the 2000 model years.

The ban was imposed as part of a sweeping set of measures intended to bring a serious air pollution problem under control. Cars older than 1997 models are also banned. The use of older vehicles is allowed only on weekends.

Quite a few other cities have banned older autos for the same reason – they were built without modern emissions controls – but motorcycles and scooters have usually been exempted.

Motorcycles and scooters are a minority of vehicles in Paris. But motorcycles have a dirty little secret, which is that where pollutants like nitrous oxide are concerned, they're worse than cars.

Day 158 – **From Motordromes to 'murderdromes'**

By 1910, motorcycles were already capable of speeds approaching 100 miles an hour. But there was really no way to capitalize on motorcycle racing as a spectator sport, as long as races were being held on public roads.

In France, however, special 'velodromes' were built for bicycle races that drew thousands of spectators. That inspired the building of America's first 'motordrome' near Los Angeles. It was a wooden track with steep banking that made for thrilling racing. Within a few years there were dozens of huge board tracks.

It was fantastically dangerous for riders, who raced in leather helmets or caps, and woolen jerseys. Guys crashed and died of *splinters*. But the end of the motordromes came after a several spectacular crashes that killed spectators. In Atlantic City, Eddie Hasha crashed, killing himself; his Indian flew into the crowd, killing several kids and injuring many. Then, in Ludlow, Kentucky, a racer named Odin Johnson crashed sending flaming wreckage into the 'stands. Eight spectators are said to have died, with many others seriously burned in the inferno.

Although board track racing continued well into the 1930s, the American national championship races were held on dirt (for reasons of safety) from 1913 onward, and newspapers decried the dangers of board track racing, calling the motordromes, 'murderdromes'.

Cool fact: The first motordrome, near Los Angeles, was not an oval; it was laid out in a circle, with a two-mile circumference.

Day 159 – **Evel's Snake River Canyon debacle**

In 1974, Evel Knievel was near the top of his fame with a problem: an audience bored with the usual death-defying feats. For years he'd suggested a Grand Canyon jump, but that's almost Federal land and the National Parks Service wanted nothing to do with him. That led him to the Snake River Canyon in Idaho.

Knievel offered the jump to ABC Sports, but they wouldn't pay his price. He then put together a business venture, with two prominent boxing and wrestling promoters, Bob Arum (of Top Rank) and Vince McMahon (World Wrestling Federation).

With other investors on board, Evel hired an aeronautical engineer to create a rocket-powered 'skycycle'. It was a missile, not a motorcycle, but that was a fine distinction.

The actual jump was, to say the least, an anticlimax. A drogue parachute that was intended to slow the rocket after landing deployed immediately upon the launch, slowing the rocket in flight. Although it almost reached the far side of the canyon, it drifted helplessly down and came to a stop pretty much directly below the launch ramp. Luckily for Evel, it missed the river; he was stuck in the harness and if he'd landed in the water he may well have drowned.

As it was, the investors got soaked. They showed the jump as a pay-per-view event at hundreds of theaters and arenas, but lost a fortune on it. Adding to the insult, the jump was pushed off the front pages of the newspapers and off the evening news when Gerald Ford pardoned Richard Nixon on the same day.

·

Day 160 – **Weirdly compelling motorcycle movie:**
12 O'Clock Boys

This is a critically acclaimed motorcycle documentary that will never, ever get the AMA's stamp of approval. Film-maker Lofty Nathan was first exposed to inner-city Baltimore's outlaw dirt-biker scene when he was in art school. He spent three years filming under near war-zone conditions, as his subjects rode and (mostly) evaded the cops on the streets of Baltimore.

Although it portrays a gang of hooligans, this is a film that brilliantly illustrates the way we all use motorcycles in a search for freedom, escape, and self-actualization.

·

Hey Buddy, can you lend me a design?

Almost every motorcycle ever made has been an iteration of some previous bike. Most improvements are incremental.

Of course, sometimes even making a little improvement feels too much like work. If you just want to make a motorcycle, and you're not fussy about making *your own*, you can license someone else's design, buy their tooling, and go straight into production.

Here are a few instances of companies that borrowed, licensed, or flat out stole whole designs. Sometimes it worked out, other times the copies were pale imitations of the originals...

Day 161 – **The Rondine**

1923: Two young Roman engineers, Carlo Gianini and Pietro Remor designed a strikingly modern four-cylinder 500cc racing motor. It featured an overhead cam and, after a few years of development, a water-cooled head. For a while, they were funded by a motorcycle-mad Count, Giovani Bonmartini. They raced it as a 'GRB'—a name created by merging their intials.

Around 1928, the Count found that racing was expensive even by the standards of minor royalty. But he owned Compagnia Nazionale Aeronautica, and he arranged for that company to acquire the assets of GRB. The young engineers had day jobs designing aircraft motors, but they continued to develop their motorcycle.

By 1934, they'd built a twin OHC version with a supercharger. It produced 86 horsepower (which would still be impressive today, from 500cc.) They called it 'Rondine', which is the Italian word for a fast-flying swallow. They needed a rider of exceptional talent to control such a rare bird, and they found one in Piero Taruffi.

In 1935, CNA was sold to a larger aeronautical enterprise. The new owners had no interest in the motorcycle racing project. Luckily Giuseppe Gilera, who was a successful Italian motorcycle maker determined to make a splash in high-level racing, acquired CNA's motorcycle assets.

The Rondine became a Gilera, and it dominated the European championship in its third guise until racing stopped for the Second World War.

Day 162 – **How do you say 'BMW' in Russian?**

The Russian Ural motorcycle—almost always seen with a sidecar—is, of course, a copy of the BMW R71. There are a variety of origin myths; I've heard that the Russians took the R71 tooling as war reparations after the war. That can't be true, because Ural production began *before* WWII. For years the Russians let people believe they'd smuggled a handful of R71s out of neutral Sweden and surreptitiously copied the design.

The reality is that Vyacheslav Molotov (one of Stalin's henchmen) and Joachim von Ribbentrop (an SS commander and Hitler confidant) negotiated a short-lived non-aggression pact in 1939. As nominal allies, the Russians simply bought a complete set of R71 plans and tooling.

By 1941, when the first Russian prototypes—dubbed M72 —were ready to go into production, the USSR was at war with Germany. To get out of German bomber range, the Russians shifted M72 production from planned factories in Moscow, Leningrad, and Kharkov to Irbit, deep in the Ural Mountains.

The motorcycle maker was known as Irbitskiy Mototsikletniy Zavod (Irbit Motorcycle Factory), which was neither romantic nor concise. I'm sure the top marketing minds in all of Communism were consulted before they settled on 'Ural'.

In total, Ural has shipped over 3,000,000 motorcycles. Many Ural owners wish that the Russians copied German metallurgy, as well as design.

Day 163 – Is a copy of a copy an original? (Answer: Nope)

Although the Urals coming off the assembly line in the 1950s were certainly not of BMW quality, the Chiang Jiang motorcycle company, in China, actually set out to copy the Ural.

The People's Liberation Army identified a need for a military motorcycle in 1950. At first, the Chinese reverse-engineered a Zundapp KS500; several thousands of those were made. But by the mid-1950s, the Soviets figured their M72 was obsolete. With nothing to lose, they offered a full set of tooling to the Chinese.

The Chiang Jiang CJ750 entered production in 1957 and variants were gradually improved, with 12V electrical systems, electric start, and overhead valves. They were produced until the early 1990s. Used ones are still advertised for sale in China, although I've read that none of them can pass the vehicle inspection required for licensing, so the only buyers are gullible foreigners.

Day 164 – **In the case of DKW, 'RT' did not mean 'retweet'…**

…Although it did go viral.

In the 1930s, the DKW factory in Zschopau, Germany made hundreds of thousands of 125cc two-strokes. The bikes were simple, cheap, and surprisingly powerful for the day. Their performance came from the improved porting, developed by Adolph Schnürle.

The DKW commuter bike was so important to the Nazi's economic plan they dubbed the model 'Reichstyp', meaning 'National Model'. That was abbreviated to RT125.

DKW exported the RT to several foreign countries. When the Nazis learned that the Dutch importer — RS Stokvis en Zonen — was owned by Jews, they forced DKW to stop supplying them with bikes. The Dutchmen commissioned Royal Enfield to make an exact copy of the RT, but the English version never worked as well because Enfield never fully understood Schnürle's two-stroke loop scavenging system.

After WWII, the Soviet Union took plans and tooling as war reparations. Zschopau was in the Eastern bloc, and they even forced ex-DKW employees to work in Russia. The Russian version was the M1A Moskva. A version was also made in Poland.

It wasn't just a Communist thing, either.

DKW's intellectual property was appropriated by BSA, which made a copy it called the Bantam. And Harley-

Davidson made an American version of the RT125 called the Hummer. The Bantam and the Hummer were both popular models. In the UK the Bantam was cheap, reliable transportation for working blokes; in the U.S. the Hummer was popular with young people.

In the chaos of the Soviet occupation of East Germany, DKW relocated to Ingolstadt, in West Germany. It began production of the RT 125W (for 'west') in 1949.

Day 165 – **Meguro copies BSA, then Kawasaki buys Meguro**

The Meguro Manufacturing Co. was one of the first Japanese motorcycle manufacturers, beginning in 1930s. Its founders were Hobuji Murato, who owned the Murato Iron Works (a company that had previously made motorcycles) and Takaji Suzuki, who was a naval officer. One of their first machines was a copy of a Motosacoche (Switzerland).

After WWII, Meguro licensed other western designs, including the BSA A7, a 500cc twin. Meguro called their version the 'Stamina' model. It was an excellent bike, with some detail changes that made it superior to the original. Meguro's products were expensive, however. With the rise of Honda, it needed a cash infusion.

In 1960, Kawasaki Heavy Industries invested in the company. A few years later, they acquired the rest of the shares. For a while bikes were sold as Kawasaki-Meguros, then they were just plain Kawasakis.

Kawasaki continued to evolve the pre-unit twins, which over time became a mechanically distinct species, although they retained a strong BSA family resemblance. You couldn't see from the outside, but Kawasaki's improvements included pressed-up cranks, one-piece con rods, and roller- and ball-bearings where the original BSA had only bushes.

None of that was enough to make the Kawasaki W1 (and later, W2) models attractive to buyers who could afford a newer, unit-construction British twin. Then, the Honda 450 dealt another blow to the biggest Kawis. By 1969, Kawasaki had pretty much stopped exporting them, although the last iteration, the W3 (with twin disc brakes) sold in the Japanese domestic market until 1974.

Day 166 – **Hardly a Harley? Or almost as good?**

At the height of the first American motorcycle boom, about half of U.S. motorcycle production was destined for export. Britain was a major market, but in 1921 the British imposed high import tariffs, to protect their own motorcycle industry.

As a result, Harley-Davidson sent Alfred Rich Child, an Englishman, to Japan. His instructions were to develop that country as an export market.

Child negotiated a distribution and parts-support agreement with the Sankyo company, and oversaw the development of an impressive dealer network; by the late '20s, there were hundreds of small Harley-Davidson dealerships scattered across the Japanese archipelago.

That sweet arrangement collapsed in 1929. One effect of the Great Depression was that the value of Japanese currency collapsed. The worthless Yen made imported Harleys prohibitively expensive.

Child then arranged for Sankyo to buy drawings and tooling, so the Japanese could make inlet-over-exhaust J-model Big Twins under license. The Americans thought it was a great deal, since the J series had just been replaced by side-valve models in the U.S.

Japanese licensing fees helped Harley survive the Depression. Meanwhile the Japanese Empire had its sights set on China. Japan ramped up its military production. Harley-Davidson unwittingly contributed to the Japanese war effort when it sent Alfred Barr to Japan for two years, to supervise the preparation of Sankyo's assembly plant in Shinagawa. Barr had been assistant factory manager in Milwaukee, and he introduced modern mass-production techniques to the Japanese.

A few years later, the Japanese plant upgraded to Harley's side-valve motors. They were sold under the Japanese name of Rikuo, which is usually translated as 'King of the Road'. That arrangement lasted until 1936 when Harley sent its man in Japan an early Knucklehead.

For whatever reason, Sankyo decided not to license that design, which precipitated a complete breakdown of the Sankyo-Harley relationship. The increasingly belligerent Japanese simply kept making Rikuos. Many were sold with a sidecar—a model popular with the Japanese military. Those had a chain drive to the rear wheel, from which a shaft drove the sidecar's wheel.

Rikuo built clones of 1930's-era Harleys until the late '50s, when they finally upgraded to a dry-sump design (similar to the Knucklehead's) and incorporated a foot-shift/hand-clutch layout. It was too little, too late, however, and the last ones were assembled in 1960.

Day 167 – **Can I borrow your scooter?**

Having been bombed into oblivion in the war, Japan needed cheap transport—preferably something that could negotiate the narrow streets of the big cities, while weaving between piles of rubble and bomb craters.

In 1946, Mitsubishi Heavy Industries developed the Silver Pigeon, a stylish scooter based closely on the Salsbury 'Motor Glide'.

The Motor Glide was made in California by E. Foster Salsbury. He used a Johnson 1½ hp motor with a CVT. Salsbury's scooters were notable for their car-like accelerator and brake pedal arrangement.

At the same time, Fuji Heavy Industries licensed the Powell scooter—as seen on American air bases in Japan—and marketed it as the 'Rabbit'.

Day 167 – **Royal Enfield**

If Harley-Davidson has a rival for its claim of being the oldest continuously-operated motorcycle company in the world, it's Royal Enfield. The distinction may hinge on whether you mean the oldest company, or the oldest brand. Because while Harley's got a continuous corporate heritage, the Royal Enfield brand changed hands—and continents—about 60 years ago.

The first Royal Enfield company was formed in England in 1901. The Enfield factory in Redditch, England, closed in 1967.

Meanwhile, back in the 1950s, the Indian government chose the 350cc Enfield Bullet for police and military use. The simple, rugged design was suited to patrolling India's rugged border regions.

In 1955, they opened a factory in Madras, where Enfield Bullets were assembled from British parts. Over the next decade they began making more and more of their own parts. When the Enfield factory closed in 1967, the Indians picked over the surplus equipment, getting everything they needed to keep producing 350 and 500cc Bullets.

They have never stopped making them. Over the years they've been subtly modernized with a disc brake and a fuel-injection system cleverly disguised as a carburetor, but the Bullet you can buy today is remarkably similar to the 1955 version the Indians chose for patrol duty in the Himalayas.

•

You might be shocked to learn…

… how old the first electric motorcycles really are.

As I write this, it seems increasingly likely that within a decade or two, ordinary motorcyclists will find themselves choosing between electric motorcycles and those powered by internal combustion.

Companies like Zero, that were formed to design and market electric motorcycles, are producing bikes that are more and more capable of competing on a level playing field (or a steeply climbing road, like the Pikes Peak International Hillclimb.) And major manufacturers are either acquiring electric vehicle companies, or designing their own EVs from scratch.

At this heady time, it's hard to remember that some of the earliest motorcycles were battery-powered.

Day 168 – **The earliest known patent**

In 1895, Ogden Bolton Jr. filed a patent for a pretty standard-looking bicycle with a DC motor integrated into the back hub. A battery was slung from the top tube. Interestingly, Bolton did not incorporate pedals (or even footpegs) in his design.

I've had trouble learning much about Bolton; he appears to have been born in England. His patent was filed in the U.S., and he died in Los Angeles. There's no record of Bolton's EV ever being produced, even as a prototype.

Day 169 – **Two rear wheels weren't twice as good**

In 1897, Hosea W. Libby filed a patent for an electric tricycle. Libby, who lived in Boston, had some ingenious ideas, such as using two motors; the second one could be switched on when a rider encountered a hill.

He also had some pretty terrible ideas. The worst was that, as his patent drawings attest, he planned to use two rear wheels set about a foot apart. Yes, it would stand upright by itself, as he proudly claimed in his patent application, but he clearly had no real understanding of way bicycles turn.

Libby also planned to use a pair of rods to connect the motor(s) to the drive wheels, although apparently later drawings show that he'd switched to a chain drive.

Day 170 – **Considering other means of transmitting power**

In 1898, Matthew J. Steffens filed a patent for an electric bicycle with a small motor behind the seat, powering a belt that ran all the way 'round the outside of the rear wheel—so the rear tire itself never touched the road. The machine ran on the belt.

That was almost certainly a terrible idea. It's hard to imagine making a belt, with the materials of the day, that would actually stay on the rear wheel.

But the next year, a guy named John Schnepf came up with an ingenious drive mechanism. In his arrangement, a small motor turned a wheel that had a direct friction drive on the rear tire. Schnepf's motor was mounted directly above the rear tire, pivoting off the cycle's center post. The weight of the battery pressed the whole apparatus down into contact with the drive wheel.

While all of these devices would, admittedly, now be described as electric bicycles (as opposed to electric motorcycles) in those early days there was essentially no difference between bicycle and motorcycle running gear.

Day 171 – **The Orwell**

'Electric Sidecar' sounds like the name of psychedelic-era rock group, or possibly a really tasty cocktail. But, it also describes the Orwell.

In the early part of the 20th century, the English firm of Ransomes, Sims and Jefferies developed an electric motorcycle, with a large battery pack carried in a sidecar. Although the vehicle did not survive, it was actually built, licensed, and tested on the road. It was dubbed 'Orwell', because the factory was located on the site of a former shipyard on the Orwell River.

Ransomes, Sims and Jefferies later sold the first gasoline-powered lawn mower. So not only did they fail to make motorcycles quieter, they actually made Saturday mornings quite a lot noisier.

Day 172 – **A Belgian Story**

In France, they have an expression *"un histoire Belge,"* which means, "a funny story." But one of the first commercially successful electric motorcycles was dreamt up by two Belgian brothers, who thought that an electric scooter would be a great way of getting around wartime fuel rationing.

Maurice and Albert Limelette designed a long, low scooter with a large battery pack in front of a small DC motor. It operated on three six-volt lead-acid batteries wired in series. The Limelettes optimistically claimed a range of 50 kilometers. It took 10 hours to recharge it.

That was enough to make it pretty popular. They sold at least a few hundred, of which several survive. The occupying German forces used some, as short-range transportation around air bases. After the war, gasoline was easier to come by and the brothers produced some stylish ICE bikes, too.

In the U.S., during the war, Merle Williams of Long Beach, CA designed and built an electric scooter that could tow a small utility trailer. Although it was not commercialized, it led him to form the Marketeer company after the war. For a while it made three-wheeled electric microcars that were so odd and minimalist that they were actually kind of cool.

Day 173 – **Science ~~Fiction~~ Fact**

Although Rollin Armer's 'Tom Swift' electric motorcycle never went into production, it deserves a mention for a few reasons. First, the builder had some serious tech credentials; he used his electric motorcycle to commute to a day job at UC Berkeley's Livermore Radiation Lab. Second, he and his bike were profiled in Cycle World in 1967. And third, Armer self-published a book explaining exactly how he'd built his EV, so he obviously hoped others would follow in his (single) track.

Armer's homebuilt project combined a curiously antique girder fork—taken from a Harley Hummer—with a custom frame, holding two Sears deep-cycle marine batteries. The motor began life as a heavy duty 'police issue' American-Bosch generator. With his modifications, it generated 38 lb-ft of torque. He devised a clever arrangement to use the batteries in series when he needed peak power, and run them in parallel when cruising on level terrain.

Armer also engineered in regenerative braking, which must've been handy on the hills around Berkeley. Even with regenerative braking, however, his homebuilt had a range of just 25 miles.

Cycle World's tester was impressed, overall. The magazine seemed to agree with the inventor when he said, "A breakthrough in battery technology would be the only thing necessary to make a real industry of electric transportation."

Armer then added, "They are always working on new batteries, and they're bound to come up with a better one someday soon."

Day 174 – **Auranthetic (whatever that means)**

The Auranthetic Charger was made in California from 1972-'79. Auranthetic Corp., brought in Taiwanese 'Gemini' mini-scramblers, without engines. They modified the frames to accept the batteries, and installed the electric components.

The bike was about the size of a contemporary Honda Ruckus, with two deep-cycle batteries that powered a 24-volt, 1 hp motor. It had a top speed of about 30 mph, and a range of about 20 miles. In some ways it was pretty primitive. Although it had what appeared to be a throttle, it really only operated at two settings.

They sold a few thousand of them; mostly two-wheelers, but there was also a trike version with a good-sized basket for cargo. Auranthetics still pop up on Craigslist from time to time, and there's a little cult of restorers. Needless to say, one popular modification is to install a more up to date motor controller.

Day 175 – **Corbin XLP 'City Bike'**

Mike Corbin is best-known for his Corbin motorcycle seat business—it's the world's foremost supplier of aftermarket motorcycle seats. But he's always had an interest in electric vehicles. When the 1973 OPEC embargo briefly triggered a gasoline shortage in the U.S., Corbin responded by designing a small electric motorcycle.

Corbin's vision was that his EV would replace gas-guzzling vehicles—at least for short urban commutes. But that didn't stop him from seeking publicity by proving that his prototype could climb up the famously steep road to the summit of Mt. Washington, NH. (That was the same road that F.O. Stanley chose to demonstrate the capabilities of his 'Stanley Steamer' car in 1899!)

Corbin produced a limited run of his XLP-1 'City Bike', and offered some for sale (notwithstanding that the 'X' stood for 'experimental'.) He claimed that it had a top speed of about 30 miles per hour, a range of 30-40 miles, and could be recharged in a few hours on regular household current. He picked up on Rollin Armer's idea for a 'two-speed' motor, running on either ½ or full voltage.

Early prototypes were fitted out with expensive silver-zinc batteries. The plan was to sell the standard models with nickel-zinc cells. The advertised price was around $1,500. The City Bike was the most-resolved EV motorcycle of the 20th century. It failed only because by the time it was ready for production, the 'oil crisis' was over.

Day 176 – **Transitron**

In 1978, the Transitron company developed a proof-of-concept electric motorcycle, the Transitron Mk.1 based on a Harley Sportster rolling chassis. The 608-pound machine carried four large batteries. They fed voltage through a proprietary control system to a DC motor which, in turn, fed power to a four-speed automatic transmission.

Steve Feher, of Transitron, sought investment from Harold Bostrom—a Milwaukee industrialist who made a fortune in tractor seats, and who was an early supporter of environmental causes (as well as a vocal advocate for population control.) Feher offered Bostrom a 25% interest in the company for $250,000. His plan was to use that money to convert a Lotus car to electric power.

I don't know whether Bostrom ponied up, but he did reach out to Brooks Stevens—a famous vehicle designer who styled the Harley-Davidson Hydra-Glide and designed the Oscar Meyer wienermobile.

The Transitron project never went anywhere. The prototype ended up in Stevens' possession. After his death, the prototype (which was still in working order) changed hands a few times. It recently sold at auction for $11,000. Unlike the motorcycle, that seems a little light.

•

Day 177 – **Worth Knowing: TT Zero**

The most prestigious electric motorcycle race in the world is the TT Zero race, held on the Isle of Man as part of the annual Isle of Man TT since 2009. (The first year the race was called TTXGP.)

The race is held over one lap of the epic 37-mile course. Lapping the TT course at over 100 miles an hour proves that the day of a true electric superbike is not far off. The record progression so far is…

- 2009 Rob Barber /AGNI 87.4 mph
- 2010 Mark Miller/MotoCzysz 96.8 mph
- 2011 Michael Rutter/MotoCzysz 99.6 mph
- 2012 Michael Rutter/MotoCzysz 104.1 mph
- 2013 Michael Rutter/MotoCzysz 109.7 mph
- 2014 John McGuinness/Mugen 117.4 mph
- 2015 John McGuinness/Mugen 119.3 mph
- 2016 Bruce Anstey/Mugen 118.4 mph

•

Day 178 – A web site worth knowing: Sideburn

www.Sideburnmag.blogspot.com is the blog associated with Sideburn magazine, an oddly charming magazine that is published in Britain but is obsessed with the American motorcycle scene – especially American flat track racing.

Sideburn is the brainchild of Gary Inman (one of the most experienced motorcycle journalists in the UK) and Ben Part. That duo's also been largely responsible for the emergence of a flat track racing series in Britain.

The Sideburn blog is not fancy, but it's often interesting and always presented with style.

•

Day 179 – **Speed thrills. Speeding tickets, not so much**

You can go onto Craigslist and buy a motorcycle for a few thousand bucks that will out-perform most six-figure Ferraris. That's great as far as affordability goes, but there's a catch: speeding tickets.

According to the National Highway Traffic Safety Administration, over 40 million speeding tickets are written every year in the U.S., at an average cost of $152 to the speeder (not counting the cost of increased insurance premiums.) Every year on average, one licensed driver in five gets a ticket.

Writing tickets is a $6 billion per year 'industry' that contributes a significant percentage of revenue in many jurisdictions. Motorcyclists contribute more than their 'fair' share.

So, anything we can do to reduce the odds of being ticketed is worthwhile, right?

There are three stages to ticket avoidance: Not getting caught, getting off with a warning, and fighting it in court —usually the last resort of a desperate rider.

To be clear: My best advice is, don't speed. My second-best advice is, don't rely on cheap paperback books for legal advice.

Day 180 – **Are radar detectors legal?**

Most vehicle-to-vehicle tickets are still based on radar readings.

The good news is, if there are vehicles ahead of you on the road, a radar detector will often warn you in time to slow down. As far as I can determine, radar detectors are legal for passenger vehicles in all states except for Virginia, and the District of Columbia. In Canada, however, radar detectors are only *permitted* in B.C., Alberta, and Saskatchewan.

The bad news is, many police radar units *detect* radar detectors.

Cops hate feeling challenged or outsmarted (and since a lot of them have a chip on their shoulder and are pretty stupid, they're often really angry.) One thing that pisses them off is realizing that you've got a radar detector — whether it's legal or not. So if you choose to use a radar detector, research the market to find one that minimizes the 'leakage' that radar detector detectors detect. (I love that last sentence!)

Day 181 – **Lidar**

LIDAR guns use an optical system to target short bursts of infra-red light. Then, the devices calculate your speed based on the rate at which the pulses are reflected back— usually off a car's front license plate, which has a special coating that makes it an excellent reflector.

There are two key points in that first paragraph. The first is, LIDAR relies on very short bursts of focused light, so a detector usually warns you too late. The second is, one of the best reflection surfaces is a front license plate, which most motorcycles don't have. This makes motorcycles harder to catch, but we're still vulnerable.

There are LIDAR jamming devices on the market. But be warned: they're illegal in California, Colorado, Illinois, Minnesota, Nebraska, Oklahoma, South Carolina, Tennessee, Texas, Utah, and Virginia as well as the District of Columbia. And again, the cops will often realize you're jamming their signal. Messing with their LIDAR readings is an excellent way to get stopped and checked for everything from up to date registration to outstanding warrants.

The best compromise it to make it harder for cops to get a 'tone' on your bike. Motorcycles don't have as many good reflective surfaces as cars to begin with. You can make your bike even stealthier by minimizing the size of your headlight, and even painting reflective surfaces with IR-absorbing Veil™ paint.

Day 182 – **The best defense is situational awareness**

Seeing the cops before they see you – giving you extra time to slow down – is always the best defense against tickets.

Like most workers, cops are lazy. They'll typically set up a speed trap where it's most likely to be productive. (Sadly this isn't usually where speeding's most dangerous to the public.) And, they'll write most tickets in places where it's easy to pull people over.

With that in mind, here's a list of situations where you should be especially vigilant.

- Any place where the speed limit suddenly drops, such as entering a school zone (where you should slow down anyway) or entering a town on a secondary highway.

- On divided highways: Any place where it's easy to cross the median.
- Overpasses. Out on the Interstate, cops will often position themselves on the tops of overpasses, where they're hard to spot but can get a reading off the back of your car. In hot weather, you should also look for them anywhere that's shady.
- The crests of hills. Don't speed up a hill, speed on the way down, when your elevated vantage point gives you a clear view of the road ahead.
- Anywhere that the traffic in front of you slows down unexpectedly.

Day 183 – **How you ride is (almost) as important as how fast you ride**

If you're weaving in between cars all herky-jerky, changing lanes without signaling, crossing the centerline, and generally riding like a hooligan, you'll get any cop's full attention right away.

If you're smooth, respectful of other drivers, and obeying all the *other* rules of the road (besides the speed limit) there's a good chance the cops won't really notice you until you've had time to see them and slow down. You're also way more likely to get the benefit of the doubt, if you're a little over the posted limit.

Smooth and fast = OK. Obnoxious and fast = ticket magnet

This brings up the question of waving to cops. There's a ton of pro and con discussion of this on web bulletin boards.

Pro: I feel that I've seen it work, either because a little wave communicates, "OK, I'll back off a tad," or maybe even makes a cop think, "He must be someone I know." Con: Sometimes, doing anything to attract attention invites a stop.

I feel that as a motorcyclist, it's sometimes appropriate to acknowledge a motorcycle cop. Don't make a big deal of it; just lift a finger. (Not the middle one!)

Day 184 – **It's fun being the lead sled dog. Until it isn't**

Although there are safety arguments for riding slightly above the median traffic speed, one of the best ways to pass through speed traps unscathed is by *not* being the fastest guy, or at least not being first in your group.

If you're passing all the traffic on the road, you're only hope is that when you come to that radar trap, there's someone already getting a ticket.

Ideally, you should find someone to act as your 'rabbit'. Let that guy pass you, then follow him at a range of 200-400 yards. (If your rabbit is another motorcyclist, you want to ensure a gap large enough that you don't look as if you're riding together. Cops write tickets all the time for whole groups of riders, based on one guy's radar reading.)

Day 185 – **Look up**

Be aware that a lot of tickets are written based on observations from airplanes. Sometimes, they're based on timing marks — heavy paint lines across the road or blocks of paint on the shoulder.

Airplane tickets are common in the wide open spaces of the Great Plains. If you see a small airplane flying parallel to the road, you should probably slow down. (It sucks that a lot of private pilots navigate by following roads, but what are you gonna' do?)

And, watch your six, too. Most of the time, you should be focused on hazards ahead of you, but you should be aware of cars that approach you from behind and which might be 'pacing' you. Another thing that sucks is, most motorcycle mirrors are next to useless, so if you're cautious about this you'll slow down for a lot of false positives.

Day 186 – **Eventually, everyone gets stopped.**

The difference between getting off with a warning and getting a ticket (or worse, arrested, or having your vehicle impounded) depends as much on what you do after being stopped.

Riders in full safety gear seem more reasonable (because they *are* more reasonable.) If you're wearing one of those skull face-masks, fingerless gloves, a t-shirt, and a back protector, and have a purple Mohawk glued to your chrome half-helmet… Oh what the fuck, if you're that guy you're probably not reading this book anyway.

But obviously, don't ride around looking like a criminal. This is especially true if you happen to be a wanted felon.

If you're caught, stop as soon as it's safe to do so. If you have time, take your helmet off. Especially if you're over 40.

Have your papers in order! When I was testing bikes for motorcycle magazines, I usually wore a hi-visibility Aerostich Roadcrafter suit, and I kept all my paperwork in a document holder on a neck chain, inside the suit. It was an arrangement that said, "I'm a professional rider." However you choose to carry them, have your driver's license, registration, and insurance accessible. Have a valid tag on your license plate. Be polite. Don't volunteer information that might incriminate you.

Cop: "Do you know how fast you were going?"

You: "No sir. I feel that I was riding with due regard for road, speed, and traffic conditions but I was not looking at my speedometer when you signaled me to stop."

Day 187 – **Fighting it**

NHTSA reports that about 5% of traffic tickets go to court. There's a lot of bullshit thrown around by guys who brag about beating tickets, but the vast majority of moving violations hold up in court. In some jurisdictions, it is virtually impossible to get a 'not guilty' verdict.

Here's some real advice: Consider just paying the ticket, even if it was for a bullshit infraction. Move on with your life. However, if you either can't afford to lose your license or are just that morally righteous, these are the three most effective techniques…

- Get a continuance. This involves going to court more than once, but the longer you can postpone your hearing, the more likely it is the cop won't show up. At that point you have a great chance of getting the ticket thrown out.
- Ask if you can have a Trial by Declaration. In many states, you're entitled to a trial by mail. You submit your claim as to why you're innocent, and the cop who wrote the ticket has to submit his claim in writing, too. Cops often get paid (even paid overtime) for court time, but this kind of paperwork is just extra work for the cop, so they often don't do it. If they don't submit their claim, you win.
- Hire a lawyer. Seriously. There are guys who specialize in speeding tickets, and they will dramatically increase your odds. They'll also dramatically increase your costs, but you may get the satisfaction of winning.

Day 188 – **To run, or not to run?**

There are jurisdictions where cops will not engage in high-speed pursuits of motorcycles. If you know that the local cops won't chase you, I suppose making a run for it is your choice.

Obviously, I don't suggest it. Unless you're really close to some great hideout. Just kidding, don't do it.

But seriously… the problem with running is that at that point, if you do get caught, you're probably going to go to jail, have your bike impounded, and possibly pick up all kinds of prison dating etiquette that, really, it would be nice to die without learning.

Now, if you are sure you've been picked up on radar by a cop traveling in the opposite direction and he can't make a U-turn for a long time, you might try gassing it to the next exit. Then, pull off and ride—not run for it—to the nearest gas station. Innocently fill up, and continue to your destination by a different route. It's imperative that you not look like you're running, to maintain a hope of deniability in the event you're caught.

I'm not advising that, mind you. I'm just saying it's worked for me.

•

Day 189 – **A web site worth knowing:
Motorcycle Classics**

www.motorcycleclassics.com is a site housing content written for the excellent Motorcycle Classics bimonthly magazine. The print edition has established itself as the American publication of record when it comes to classic bikes.

Motorcycle Classics has a wealth of well-organized information on hundreds of vintage bikes, including a virtual tour of the Barber Museum that is quite a bit more useful than the Barber's own site.

Cool fact: Motorcycle Classics is published out of an office in the unlikely city of Topeka, Kansas. The publisher's other titles include specialty magazines for beekeepers and chicken farmers.

•

Day 190 – *Zen and Art of Motorcycle Maintenance*

Only one book about motorcycles has ever really become a mainstream bestseller: *Zen and Art of Motorcycle Maintenance: An Inquiry into Values*, by Robert Pirsig.

'Zen' first appeared in 1974. It's been in print continuously ever since. It's sold over 5,000,000 copies. To this day it seems that every time I look around in a crowded airport waiting lounge, someone's reading this dense 418-page tome.

Or should I say, "trying to read it"? Because let me tell you, it's heavy going. While there are some beautiful descriptions of riding, and some insightful observations about motorcycle maintenance, they're interspersed amongst interminable, introspective monologues.

Everyone has one friend like this: He is really intelligent but sadly completely full of himself, and to make matters worse, he either can't tell or doesn't care when people are obviously bored with whatever two-hour-long story he's telling – probably a story he's already told you anyway. Yeah, well... Pirsig is that guy.

Is spite of the book's flaws, when a stranger hears that you ride motorcycles, they'll still ask, "Have you read 'Zen and the Art of Motorcycle Maintenance'?"

I did read it, so you don't have to. Here are eight things you need to know to discuss it intelligently.

Day 191 – **Robert M. Pirsig**

Robert Maynard Pirsig was born in Minneapolis in 1928. His father was a lawyer who taught law and was later the dean of a law school. As kid, Pirsig was very precocious—definitely what we'd now call a gifted child.

Although he entered university to study science, he had a difficult time as a student. He was expelled, and enlisted in the U.S. Army; he served in Korea from 1946- '48. After his discharge, he studied Eastern Philosophy. For a time, he lived and studied in India. He continued to bounce around as a student, and had a fractious few years at the University of Chicago, before landing a teaching position in Bozeman, Montana.

He was still a relatively young man (in his early 30s) when he was treated in mental institutions for a diagnosis that included paranoid schizophrenia and clinical depression. Those were the days of electroshock therapy.

Ten years later (around 1970) Pirsig had the most menial writing job there is, writing computer manuals. In his spare time, he started writing *Zen and the Art of Motorcycle Maintenance*.

Day 192 – **You think you've dealt with rejection**

By his own count, Pirsig submitted his manuscript to 121 publishers. According to the Guinness Book of Records, that's the most rejections ever by a book that went on to be a bestseller.

One lone editor, at the publishing house William Morrow, offered a standard $3,000 advance. He said the book forced him to decide what he was in publishing for. He warned Pirsig that he should not expect any additional payment.

Thankfully, before it was published in 1974, it had been dramatically shortened. The original manuscript was 800,000 words.

Day 193 – **Synopsis**

The book describes a 17-day journey that the narrator (a character much like Pirsig) takes from Minnesota to the west coast. He's accompanied by his son, riding pillion. For much of the journey, they are also accompanied by a couple, their friends John and Sylvia Sutherland.

That short summary can make the book seem like a classic road trip story, and it does have those elements; descriptions of riding, of scenery, and of the usual bike trouble. But the journey is really a framework for Pirsig's long philosophical essays, which he calls 'chautauquas', on the topic of 'quality'.

Day 194 – **Philosophy**

'Zen' blends eastern mysticism with classical Greek philosophy. While those chautauquas are heavy going, they're not pseudo-philosophy, they're real philosophy— in the sense that Pirsig lays out a coherent definition what's true and good.

In fact, the two motorcycle riders portrayed in the book represent two fundamental ways of approaching the universe. The narrator seeks to understand, while his riding buddy is satisfied with merely experiencing life.

Day 195 – **What bike did he ride?**

The motorcycle that the narrator rides is never clearly identified in the book. But at the time he was formulating the ideas that went into the book, Pirsig made a very similar road trip on a 1964 Honda CB77 Superhawk.

The 305cc CB77 was a bestseller in its own right for Honda, from 1961-'68. When it hit the market, it was Honda's largest-displacement production motorcycle.

Pirsig kept his Superhawk forever (or at least, I've seen references to him still owning it as recently as 2007.

The other motorcycle in the book was a BMW R60/2, which was inspired by a bike owned by a real-life riding buddy. That motorcycle has changed hands a few times, too, but it's still known to exist.

Day 196 – **Later life**

The book secured Pirsig's financial future. Shortly after it was published, he received a Guggenheim Fellowship, and he began working on a 'sequel', called *Lila: An Inquiry into Morals*. In spite of his success, Pirsig remained plagued by depression. He lived in New England as a near-hermit.

If you read a recent edition of 'Zen', you'll find a tragic afterword, describing the death of his son Chris, who is a major character in the book. He was murdered in a botched robbery in San Francisco, as he was leaving a Zen center.

At the time, Pirsig was over 50. He had remarried and his wife Nell was pregnant. They'd planned to have an abortion (presumably, Pirsig felt he was too old to become a new father.) When Chris was murdered, they changed their plan and had a daughter, who Pirsig felt was Chris' reincarnation. Years later, Pirsig reentered psychotherapy. His doctor identified a chemical imbalance, prescribed drugs, and Pirsig's depression disappeared.

Day 197 – **If you really want to read it ...**

If my Executive Summary, presented above, isn't satisfying, and you really want to plow through the whole book on your own, I recommend the companion volume— *Guidebook to Zen and the Art of Motorcycle Maintenance*, by Ron DiSanto and Tom Steele. Pirsig himself approved of their work.

You can also visit a web site: http://www.venturearete.org, which offers a sort of 'beginner's guide' to Pirsig's work.

Day 198 – **Pirsig Pilgrims, like author Mark Richardson**

Pirsig's route, from Minneapolis to San Francisco via Yellowstone National Park, covers 2,100 miles. Retracing his voyage is, apparently, a thing people still do. In fact, if you open up a Google search window and type 'map of Pirsig's route' you'll find a bunch of links with route info you can print off.

Or, you can stay home by the fireplace and read Mark Richardson's 'Zen and Now: On the Trail of Robert Pirsig and the Art of Motorcycle Maintenance'. In the early 2000s, Richardson retraced Pirsig's journey and wrote an account that's a heck of a lot easier to read than the original! Highly recommended.

Day 199 – **Investment Grade: The world's most valuable motorcycles**

If you can believe the website Gizmag—and who wouldn't? If it's on the Internet it must be true, right? — the collectible motorcycle market is considerably undervalued, compared to other 'investments of passion'.

I believe it. In the top tier, collector cars now command prices about 100x those of the most desirable motorcycles. One of the most valuable motorcycles ever sold at auction was a 1910 Winchester, which sold for well over half a million bucks. That suggests that the association with firearms encouraged a gun collector to spend at least five times what any motorcycle-only collector would have spent.

And a recent survey of the Top 100 motorcycle auction prices included no less than seven bikes that had belonged to Steve McQueen. One was a Husqvarna 400 that sold for about 100 times what it would have been worth on Craigslist. Experts on the valuation of collectibles see the huge premium paid for McQueen's bikes as evidence that the motorcycle market is still immature. That's good for you, in the sense that all else being equal, your old bikes have lots of room to increase in value.

One thing that's interesting is that so far, virtually no Japanese motorcycles have become top-grade investments. That survey of the Top 100 auction prices, didn't include a single Jap bike. (The authors did note that an ex-Jim Redman Honda RC164 250cc six-cylinder Grand Prix bike was offered at a price that would have made it the most valuable motorcycle of all time. It failed to meet its reserve.)

For a relatively up to date list of the top prices paid at auction, drop by The Vintagent's excellent blog.

So what marques offer the best investment potential? At the top end, the indications are clear…

Day 200 – #11—Hildebrand & Wolfmüller

Their 'motorrad' was pretty ingenious, with a parallel-twin motor mounted horizontally, so that the connecting rods acted directly on the rear wheel, which served as the flywheel and crankshaft. Even the pushrods that actuated the valves were driven directly by the rear wheel.

That arrangement meant rear wheel speed and engine rpm were one and the same. You could only stop the machine by stopping the motor.

That might seem like a real inconvenience, but this German company was the first commercially successful motorcycle manufacturer. It's likely that at least 1,000 customers bought Hildebrand & Wolfmüller bikes in the mid-1890s.

Day 201 – #10—Iver Johnson

The Worcester, MA company produced motorcycles from 1907 until 1916. They made a 4.5 hp single and an 8 hp v-twin. Iver Johnson were early adopters of chain drive (at a time when many motorcycles relied on belts, which were prone to slipping and needed frequent adjustment.) The twin was also available with a two-speed rear hub.

Day 202 – #9—Henderson

William and Tom Henderson started producing four-cylinder motorcycles in Detroit in 1912. From the start, they were renowned for smooth power and reliability (the motorcycles, not Bill and Tom). Police forces wanted them, because they were the fastest vehicles on the road.

In 1917, the brothers sold out to Ignaz Schwinn (of bicycle fame). Schwinn made and sold both Henderson and Excelsior motorcycles until 1931.

Henderson motorcycles weren't just popular in the U.S. They were exported around the world, to the point that now, about half of all surviving Hendersons are owned by foreign collectors.

Day 203 – #8—Flying Merkel

Joseph Merkel produced his first motorcycle engine in 1902 and began making entire motorcycles in '03. Over the next few years, he merged his business with Light Manufacturing and Foundry, of Pottstown PA. That company was then acquired by Miami Cycle and Manufacturing, and Merkel relocated to its Middletown OH plant.

Through it all, Merkel insisted on high-quality components that ensured his motorcycles were among the best on the market. In 1911, Miami launched the Flying Merkel brand. Joseph Merkel stayed with the company until 1914; they sold 'Flying Merkels' for another year.

In the days before oil pumps, riders had to remember to hand-pump oil from a tank into a total loss system. (Then, down the road, they had to stop and drain their crankcases.) Merkel invented an oil pump that operated off the throttle. It was later copied by Harley and Indian.

About 50 are thought to still exist.

Day 204 – #7—Ducati

Some of the newest motorcycles to have reached the top tier of 'investment grade' collector bikes are Ducatis. The caveat here is that the Italian marque is makes Gizmag's 'Top 100' list on the strength of two almost-new motorcycles.

A few years ago, Ducati auctioned off an ex-Casey Stoner GP10 factory MotoGP racer, and an ex-Rossi GP11 model. Both sold for well over $300k. Some early 1970's bevel twins also command high prices.

Day 205 – #6—Indian

Five Indians made the 'Top 100' list, so the iconic brand clearly has investment potential. Among the rarest and most valuable ones are early board-track racers, which had surprisingly powerful eight-valve motors and were capable of top speeds around 100 miles an hour—shocking in the years before the First World War.

If you think you've found one, be careful; there are now so many replica parts floating around that it's possible to build an entire Indian board track racer out of new spares.

Day 206 – #5—BMW

The highest price ever paid for a BMW was a 1939 'Kompressor' 500cc race bike. That was the dominant motorcycle in the last year or two before WWII—so much so that after the war, the FIM banned forced induction.

Stripped of its supercharger, a similar motorcycle—the Rennsport production racer—was sold in the early- to mid-'50s. Those too have now climbed into six-figure territory.

Day 207 – #4—Crocker

Albert Crocker only made about 200 motorcycles, but seven of them made Gizmag's "Top 100" prices list. That gives you some idea of the incredible mystique of this brand.

Crocker was a pal of Oscar Hedstrom and Charles Hendee, of Indian fame. He briefly owned a motorcycle shop in Kansas City before moving to Los Angeles. In 1931 he made his first race bike, but his fame rests on the big twins he made beginning in '36.

His bikes were 'hemis'—and so powerful that he offered a refund, should any customer ever lose a top-speed competition to a stock Harley or Indian! They were expensive, even at the height of the Depression, but it was WWII that ultimately killed off the Crocker brand.

Day 208 – #3—Harley-Davidson

If you look across the board at the 'Top 100' prices paid at auction, you can't help but notice that American bikes account for a disproportionate share. That weighting reflects two things: first that in the early years of motorcycling, there were a lot of American brands creating a lot of innovative motorcycles; and second, the U.S. is home to a large number of wealthy collectors who, it seems, like to buy American.

Of course, as 'the' American brand, a number of Harleys have commanded top prices. The most inherently valuable Harleys are early 'strap tank' singles and the first twins. That said, many of the Harleys that commanded the highest prices at auction were newer and more common models that had been owned by celebrities from Marlon Brando to the Pope.

Day 209 – #2—Vincent HRD

Some time time in the early 1930s, Phil Irving was working at his drafting table when he accidentally overlaid two drawings of 500cc single-cylinder motors. He realized that he could make a 1000cc twin, and the Series A 'Rapide' motor was born. (Or at least, conceived. And as we're told, life begins at conception.)

Between 1936 and '55, Irving's 'Vincent' company produced about 6,000 motorcycles, of which about half are still known to exist. In spite of being relatively 'common', 14 are on that list of the 100 highest prices paid at auction.

Interestingly, the most valuable Vincent of all is not on Gizmag's list of top auction prices. That's because the last time Rollie Free's land-speed record-setting Vincent changed hands, it was in a private sale. (The price, was rumored to be $1.1 million.)

Day 210 – #1—the most valuable brand of all...

George Brough began making his 'Brough Superior' motorcycles in England in 1919. He advertised them as

"The Rolls-Royce of motorcycles." That naturally caught the attention of Charles Stewart Rolls and Sir Frederick Royce, who worried about their trademark being used in such a fashion.

As the story goes, Rolls-Royce sent a man to Nottingham. The car company's emissary saw workers wearing white gloves assembling motorcycles in a pristine workshop. He returned, and said, "Yes, they are the Rolls-Royce of motorcycles," at which point Chuck and Fred were, like, "OK, then."

Between 1919 and 1940, Brough produced about 3,000 motorcycles—virtually every one 'bespoke', which is to say made to a buyer's specification. Of those, about 1,000 are still in existence.

Brough Superiors dominate Gizmag's 'Top 100' list with 24 bikes. The Vintagent's list of most-valuable bikes is also heavy with Broughs. One thing that's interesting about those lists is, at the very top you find a bunch of totally unique bikes; factory racers, or bikes that were owned by celebrities. But any old Brough Superior is valuable (the same's largely true for Vincents.) Even models that were produced in large(ish) numbers, such as the SS100, command solid six-figure prices.

•

Day 211 – **A web site worth knowing: Pashnit**

www.pashnit.com is the only site I've included in this book that operates (partly) on a $20 subscription basis. It's also very California-centric. Still, if you live in (or plan to visit) California, that 'Jackson' will buy you a year's access to the best database of riding roads imaginable.

Pashnit is the creation of Tim Mayhew, who also leads guided motorcycle tours around the state. He's become a vastly experienced sport-tourer, and besides planning routes, his web site is a great place to buy accessories, learn, and connect with like-minded riders.

•

You don't know what you've got 'til it's gone

In the last section, I listed bikes that most of us will never own. (If you are in the market for any of those most-coveted, investment-grade machines, will you lend me the money I need to renovate my house instead?)

But there's another kind of motorcycle 'investment': Bikes that come onto the market—often to fanfare—but which were then largely rejected by consumers. Those models are then discontinued (at least in the U.S.) making them rare here. Years later, they come to be appreciated and their values appreciate, too.

Here's a series of bikes that launched as moto-magazine cover stories but flopped in the marketplace. Some are now full-on classics, but most of the newer ones are still available as ordinary used bikes on Craigslist.

Day 212 – **Münch Mammoth**

Friedl Münch worked for Horex, a German motorcycle manufacturer, until it went out of business in 1956. After that Münch ran his own tuning shop. In 1966, one of his clients requested an exceptional motorcycle. That commission was, effectively, the first Münch Mammoth.

Münch took a 996cc four-cylinder NSU car engine and fitted in a frame reminiscent of a Norton Featherbed (on steroids!) The resulting motorcycle was not as heavy as you might think (less than 500 pounds.) Even though that first version was already powerful by '60s standards, by the time Münch got into anything resembling serial production, he'd opted for a 1,200cc motor.

Floyd Clymer invested in the company and had high hopes of bringing the expensive muscle cruiser to the U.S. market, but it never caught on. Not because it was too big, but because it seemed fantastically expensive. It cost nearly $4,000; about twice the price of a BMW R69S (which was, otherwise, the most expensive of the German imports.)

It's interesting to realize think that the $4,000 price tag, which seemed excessive in the late '60s, is actually 'only' the equivalent of about $27,000 today. So the Mammoth would not nearly be the most expensive bike on the market today.

In the present day, a runner would go for about $60k. That means that if you'd sprung for it in 1968, it would have performed about as well as the U.S. stock market. And have been more fun.

Day 213 – **The Vetter Mystery Ship**

Craig Vetter made a fortune selling aftermarket fairings, at a time when virtually all motorcycles came devoid of any kind of wind or weather protection. In 1980 (about ten years after the last Mammoth was carefully hand-crafted) Vetter launched his one and only entire motorcycle: The Mystery Ship.

Vetter started with an entire Kawasaki KZ1000. He modified the frame, fitted it with trick magnesium wheels and a full Yoshimura exhaust system. But the signature element of the Mystery Ship was full bodywork; either stunning or weird, depending on your point of view.

This was another machine that had a lot to recommend it, but was killed in the market by sticker shock. Vetter hoped to go into production, but couldn't even sell out the first run of ten motorcycles. At $10,000, it was more than triple the price of a KZ1000 with largely similar performance. Vetter offered a variety of engine upgrades for even more money, and at least one was sold with a turbocharger system created by RC Engineering.

Although riders rejected Vetter's creation, it might have helped to inspire other builders, such as Bimota. Stylists at Honda followed some of his cues on the CX500, and Hans Muth might've had it in mind when he sketched his brilliant Suzuki Katana.

As recently as 2009, Mystery Ships were still occasionally cropping up on Craigslist and eBay. Back then, they were going for $25,000 or so.

Day 214 – **Ducati Paso 750**

In the mid-1980s, Ducati had a good motor in the form of the Ducati Pantah 750, but the company was getting hammered by the Japanese brands.

In response, Cagiva (which owned Ducati at the time) hired Massimo Tamburini to create a new bike based on the Pantah motor. Tamburini's design — featuring fully enclosed bodywork — was revealed at the Turin bike show in 1985. They called it the 'Paso', in honor of a great Italian motorcycle racer, Renzo Pasolini.

Ducati had high hopes for the Paso, which was available in the 1986 model year. Unfortunately, it turned out to be strikingly similar to the Honda Hurricane which came out at about the same time. It was expensive and underpowered—especially compared to the new Suzuki GSX-R750.

Ducati only sold about 4,000 of them, and gave up on it after 1988. (Although the same styling was carried over onto the 906 for another few years.) If you find one today, you may be challenged when it comes to sourcing good 16" tires, but it's a rideable Tamburini masterpiece.

Day 215 – **Yamaha SRX**

At a time when Honda, Suzuki and Yamaha were all introducing fire-breathing four-cylinder sport bikes, Yamaha hedged its bet, and installed the big, single-cylinder motor from the XT600 trail bike into a light, sporty street chassis.

The result was the 1986 Yamaha SRX. Frank Melling called it the best British bike ever made in Japan. What he meant was that the SRX was the heir to thumpers like the BSA Gold Star or even the Norton Manx.

Although it sold well in Europe, it was never popular in the U.S. Yamaha imported it one year only, and they're now snapped up by cognoscenti the moment they appear on Craigslist.

Day 216 – **BMW K1**

The K1 is another bike, like the Paso, that is all about that full bodywork. In the late '80s, BMW faced European Union regulations that would limit motorcycles to 100 horsepower. And yet, the Germans wanted a bike capable of cruising at 150 miles an hour on the autobahn.

BMW responded by designing the K1, based on the four-cylinder K100 'flying brick' motor. It had the lowest drag coefficient of any production motorcycle, which caused heat buildup problems in early versions. Add to this, it had weight issues brought on by the extensive bodywork (and the way BMW's design team and engineers kept adding features.) The K1 was also hurt by U.S. emissions controls, which further cut power to 95 hp. Last but not least, in a recurring theme in this chapter, it was too expensive at $13,000.

Although it had a six-year production run, from 1988-'93, BMW sold less than 7,000 units. Even now, it's got love-it-or-hate-it looks, and the riding experience can't be compared to other sports-tourers, but its got enough fans to ensure classic status.

Day 217 – **Honda NT650 Hawk GT**

The 1980s was a decade of stunning creativity in the motorcycle industry. Some bikes that came of age then—Gixxers and Ninjas leap to mind—have continued to evolve all the way to the present day. Other '80s designs that were perhaps as good or better didn't click with American consumers.

The Honda Hawk GT was one of the latter group. It was the second Honda, after only the RC30, to get the elf-inspired Pro-Arm single-sided swingarm. But the 650cc twin made less than 60 hp, so it found itself in a sort of nether-market; a little too expensive for beginners but not fast enough for experts.

Except that it was, or at least… it could be. It was the machine that made the Erion brothers' reputation as race tuners and in many ways paved the way for bikes like the Ducati Monster and Suzuki's now-venerable SV650.

Honda sold the closely related Bros models in the Japanese domestic market for years, and sold the similar (but shaft-drive) Revere model in Europe for longer, too. But the Hawk GT only came to the U.S. from 1988-'91. It's a total 'cult' bike.

Day 218 – **Honda Transalp**

This was an adventure bike, long before motorcyclists realized that was a category. It was sold in other places before it came to the U.S. in 1989, and continued to be sold elsewhere long after American Honda gave up on it in '91.

That said, it has a lot to recommend it. It's comfortable, has great weather protection, and reasonable (if uninspiring) performance. The Transalp is definitely a road-biased adventure bike, but Cycle World described it as, "[I]n short, a terrific motorcycle for those of us who have to make what may be the ultimate compromise: ownership of just one motorcycle."

If you're looking for the motorcycle equivalent of a Leatherman tool, this is it. And it's definitely going to hold its value as it transitions from 'cult' to 'collector' status.

Day 219 – **Honda GB500 'Tourist Trophy'**

Joni Mitchell could have sung, "You don't know what you've got 'til it's gone" about the GB500.

Honda first sold a 400cc version in the mid-'80s in Japan, but the 500 single, with a motor based on the XL600 trail bike, came out a few years later. The street bike had 19" front/18" rear spoked wheels, clip-ons, and a solo seat. It came in one color: British racing green. It evoked bikes like the AJS 7R and BSA Gold Star, hence the 'Tourist Trophy' model name.

Honda imported it to the U.S. 1989 through '90, but dealers didn't know how to sell it. In fact, there were still 1,000 new ones in the U.S. in 1992, that were re-exported to Germany!

Now, there are at least a thousand guys in the U.S. who wish those bikes had stayed in this market.

Day 220 – **Yamaha TDM 850**

Yamaha's American managers should probably have learned from Honda's Transalp experience, but they didn't. Yamaha tried to create an American demand for the similar (but more powerful) TDM 850. They gave up after only two years; it was imported to the U.S. in 1992-'93 only.

The motor is a parallel twin with the 'Genesis' five-valve head. With a wide handlebar and long-travel suspension, it was (and is!) a terrific real-world touring bike. It soaks up potholes and comfortably handles gravel roads.

The British motorcycle paper MCN said of it, "Fairly revolutionary when launched and certainly years ahead of its time." It was ahead of its time, at least as far as American riders were concerned. After Yamaha gave up on it here, an even way cooler version was sold in Europe, with a 270-degree crank.

If you can find one, it's still a great adventure bike for the paved roads that most of us stick to.

Day 221 – **Yamaha GTS1000**

In the early '90s, Yamaha really took a chance with the GTS1000 sports tourer. The first feature you notice is the RADD front end — it's one of the handful of modern bikes without a conventional fork. But it also featured the Genesis head, electronic fuel injection, and ABS.

None of those things were 'normal' in 1993 when it was introduced to the U.S. market. Riders didn't quite know what to make of it; it was fairly heavy, and pretty expensive. Yamaha only brought it to the U.S. for two years.

As underwhelming as those initial sales were, it probably made the transition from being merely 'used' to being 'collectible' faster than almost any other bike. By 2006, Bike magazine had listed it as one of the '50 coolest bikes of all time'. A few years after that, it appeared as a 'Smart Money' selection in Motorcyclist.

If you ever see one, buy it. It's still a rideable sport tourer, and a guaranteed future museum piece.

Day 222 – **Moto Guzzi Sport 1100**

In the mid- '90s, Moto Guzzi released the Sport 1100, built up on a spine frame inspired by the famous 'Dr. John' Wittner's BOTT race bike. The bike was long, heavy, and really not that powerful. But torque and top flight suspension components went a long way towards hiding the weight.

It was sold from '95 to 2000, first as a carbureted bike and later with fuel injection. I suppose from a marketing point of view, the problem was that customers wanted it to be an alternative to a Ducati 916, which was never on the cards.

That said, it's robust, easy to maintain, and deceptively fast. The people who have them, love them. This is a bike that's near the bottom of its price curve, and is both fun to ride and a good investment.

Day 223 – **Suzuki TL1000S**

The British magazine MCN called this ferocious twin "the Freddie Kreuger of biking".

The problem with the TL1000S was that in order to package the long motor in an acceptable (for a sport bike) wheelbase, Suzuki used an innovative rotary damper in the rear shock. It wasn't up to the task, and the motor's massive torque output shifted a lot of weight to the rear at the best of times. That set up chassis instability which, in turn, exacerbated front-end instabilities. Even the hardened ex-racer types who write magazine tests were put off by it. It was only produced from 1997 to 2001.

Savvy owners invested in better steering dampers, and in time, aftermarket companies produced better shocks for the TL. Still, almost 20 years later, it remains a bike that even experts approach with caution. Historically badass bikes make good investments though, so if you see one that's intact and complete, buy it.

Day 224 – **Kawasaki W650**

It feels a little weird to include a faux-vintage retro bike in this group, but Kawasaki's W650 is a special case.

Kawasaki introduced this 650cc vertical twin in 1999. Although its style evoked British twins from the '60s (as well as Kawasaki's own bikes from that period) the W650 had a Ducati-style bevel drive to the overhead cam. The bike didn't just have retro style, it had a 72mm bore and an 80mm stroke. Those measurements were about 30 years out of date, giving the motor an authentic vibe.

It was imported into the U.S. in 2000 and 2001, but Kawasaki's American managers didn't have the stomach to compete with Triumph's new-again Bonneville at that time. Too bad; many experts believe that Kawasaki was the company that got its retro right. It only took 13 years for the magazine Motorcycle Classics to profile it.

Day 225 – **Wild Card: Aprilia Moto 6.5**

In the mid- '90s, Aprilia set out to create a motorcycle that would appeal to the sort of non-riding urban types we came to call 'metrosexuals'. (But really, who hasn't had sex in the metro? Isn't that everyone?)

They called Philippe Starck—a French product designer who was more at home sketching kitchenware. Starck had a free hand, wrapping a strikingly modern(istic) motorbike around the Rotax 650cc single-cylinder motor from the Aprilia Pegaso dual-sport.

Motorcycle magazines snickered. Non-riders were fascinated, but they weren't sufficiently interested to go to the trouble of getting a motorcycle permit. So sales languished, perhaps undeservedly; the Moto 6.5 is actually a pretty functional urban commuter with some interesting touches like the eccentric chain adjuster. One challenge: the striking bodywork is simply unavailable these days.

Although I don't believe this model was ever imported into the U.S., it got a boost in credibility when it was featured in The Art of the Motorcycle at the Solomon R. Guggenheim Museum in New York in 1998.

•

Day 226 – **A web site worth knowing: Occhio Lungo**

https://occhiolungo.wordpress.com/ is a terrific personal blog written by Pete Young, who is one of the most experienced restorers and riders of pioneer-era motorcycles. 'Occhio lungo' is an Italian expression that literally means 'long eye' but is used to describe a person who has seen plenty, and may use their superior knowledge to mess with your head!

I suppose you should take that as a warning. In Pete's own words...

I'm a fan of the earliest motorcycles circa 1860s-1920s. The website shows early machines being ridden as their makers intended, on events like the Motorcycle Cannonball, The Pioneer Run, the Irish National Rally, the Bud Ekins Memorial Tour and other special events.

I like to focus on the oddest machines, especially ones who used different designs than the more successful manufacturers (engineering evolutionary dead-ends!) But also the early adopters of tech like disc brakes, telescoping forks, monoshocks, transverse 4 cylinders, etc. that were all around pre1910, only to disappear for 50 years before becoming popular again.

The writing is dry, but the love of the bikes can sometimes make up for that. Posts are sporadic, as I get time when not riding or repairing my bikes in the workshop. Photos are my own and are often the only place to see 100+ year old bikes actually on the road instead of in a museum. Workshop sessions are sometimes featured as the bikes do tend to break down regularly!

•

Day 227 – **Why bother with R&D? Just steal someone else's idea**

Behind the Iron Curtain, Soviet-style centralized 'planned' economies put almost all their engineering talent to work on military projects. As a result, civilian vehicle production lagged and development was almost nonexistent. Look up the East German 'Trabant' car for an example of just how ghastly their vehicles were. As bad as they were, ordinary workers still had to wait years to get one.

Motorcycle racing was fantastically popular in Communist countries. In the postwar period, the East German Grand Prix drew hundreds of thousands of fans. They had a domestic brand to root for, because there was an exception to the general technological backwardness of the Communist Bloc: The East German MZ Grand Prix team. 'MZ' stood for Motorradwerk Zschopau, which is translates as 'Zschopau motorcycle factory'.

Beginning in 1953, the MZ race shop was under the command of one of the true geniuses of our sport—Walter Kaaden.

Day 228 – Walter who?

Walter Kaaden's father had worked for DKW. Young Walter attended his first race at the famous Nurburgring race course when he was eight. He went on to study at the Chemnitz Technical Academy. During WWII, he worked on the Nazi rocket programs.

Kaaden was briefly interned by the Americans at the end of the war. Many of the Nazi's rocket guys were spirited away to U.S. missile programs but Kaaden stayed in East Germany. For a while, after the war, he had a business building wooden roof trusses, which were obviously in high demand in bombed-out postwar Germany.

He came to the attention of the IFA motorcycle factory when his privateer DKW RT125 was faster than the IFA's factory racer bikes. Kaaden took over the IFA race department in 1953, and then IFA was re-launched as MZ —part of East Germany's centrally-planned Communist industrial strategy.

Unlike many of that country's citizens who were held in check by one of the world's most feared secret police services, he appears to have been an enthusiastic, life-long supporter of the Communist regime.

Day 229 – **The inventor of the expansion chamber exhaust**

After superchargers were banned from Grands Prix, Kaaden developed MZ two-strokes that combined disc valve induction with expansion chamber exhausts. The exhausts, in particular, were essentially Kaaden's invention. (There were some pre-Kaaden exhausts that took the general bulbous shape, but he was the first person to really understand the principles of resonance, pressure waves and all the stuff that made them work.)

It is impossible to overstate the engineering impact of the expansion chamber. In 1954, MZ engines produced about 100bhp per liter. By 1961, they produced 200bhp per liter.

Day 230 – **Commie Propaganda**

The success of MZ in Grand Prix racing figured prominently in East German propaganda. While the marque was justifiably proud that the very best riders of the day (Hailwood included) lined up to ride their 125 and 250cc racers, they also groomed a homegrown Communist star in the form of Ernst Degner.

Degner was born in Poland, but his family fled into Germany to avoid the advancing Russian army. They obviously stopped too soon, because he grew up in East Germany. After training as a mechanic and engineer, he quickly showed a lot of promise as a motorcycle racer in the German Democratic Republic.

In March of 1956, Degner started working for Kaaden at MZ. He was utterly dominant in national competition, and by 1958 the Communist Party allowed MZ to enter him in all the World Championship races. He scored his first Grand Prix victory at Monza in 1959.

Day 231 – **Degner Defects!**

The Berlin Wall went up in August, 1961. Ernst Degner realized that if he and his family were going to get out of East Germany, they had to move fast.

His opportunity arose at the Swedish Grand Prix in Kristianstad. Degner's MZ broke—or perhaps I should say, he purposely broke his bike—early in the race. Degner hopped in his car and drove to Denmark, from where he took a ferry to West Germany. He met up with his wife and family; they'd also managed to get from East to West Germany.

It's often believed that Degner defected and went straight to Japan, but that's not what really happened. He originally went from MZ to EMC, a West German motorcycle company. Degner moved to Hammamatsu, Japan to work for Suzuki a few months later, at the end of 1961.

Day 232 – **Suzuki suddenly succeeds**

Over the winter, Degner designed new 50cc and 125cc road racers for Suzuki. Stories are told that Degner escaped with a full set of drawings, or even a complete motor, but they're probably exaggerated. Degner was a trained engineer and a confidant of Kaaden. Everything he needed was in his head. Needless to say, the new Suzukis looked a lot like the old MZs.

Degner won the 50cc World Championship for Suzuki in 1962. His old mentor, Walter Kaaden, never forgave him.

Day 233 – **Kaaden wasn't the only one who got burned**

Degner raced in multiple classes for Suzuki from 1962-'66. He won a total of 10 races, but the low point came in the final race of the 1963 season, at Suzuka.

Degner crashed in the 250cc race, and his motorcycle caught on fire. He was severely burned, and required many painful skin grafts.

At the end of his racing career, he returned to West Germany, where he worked in technical capacity for Suzuki.

Day 234 – **A death, certainly. A mystery? Maybe.**

Degner was addicted to pain meds. He eventually moved to Tenerife, in the Canary Islands, where he ran a car rental business. That's where he died, in 1983. He was only 51 years old.

The cause of death was thought to be a drug overdose. He suffered from depression, and may have committed suicide. It's also possible that he was murdered by the Stasi (the East German secret police) in revenge for his defection.

•

Day 235 – **A web site worth knowing: ADVrider**

www.advrider.com aka Adventure Rider is the largest dual sport/adventure discussion board by miles (millions and millions of 'em, put up by hundreds of thousands of riders from around the world.)

It's not a fancy curated site, it's just a forum, but the sheer magnitude of content is mind-boggling. There are thousands and thousands of 'Ride Reports' dating back to 2001. Most, of course, are mundane… but there are more than a few epic descriptions of life-affirming adventures.

Although it's mostly focused on the dual sport/adventure scene, the community of contributors is large, active, and has a diverse set of interests, ranging from scooters to MotoGP.

•

Great motorcycle songs

Pop music and motorcycles are all about coming of age, the pursuit of freedom and happiness, and rebellion. No wonder there have been so many great pop songs about motorcycles!

Day 236 – **Not Number 1:** *Bat Out of Hell*

One motorcycle journalist dissed this Meat Loaf (or is it 'Meatloaf'?) classic by describing it as the longest song ever to end in a low-side crash. In its favor, of course, is the motorcycle graphic on the album cover.

Bat Out of Hell was a massive hit in the late '70s. Why is not worthy of being #1? Well, Mr. Loaf is about five minutes into the song before there's a definitive motorcycle reference. And then, there's the matter of whether or not Mr. Loaf actually rides.

Although he owns a couple of bikes, and has been photographed on motorcycles, there's a YouTube video of Mr. Loaf sitting on one of his bikes, in his garage, explaining that that's all he does. Seriously, he just sits on them and never, ever rides them.

Why would anyone even admit to that?

Day 237 – *Leader of the Pack* **by the Shangri-Las**

The Shangri-Las were a girl group from New York. They released *Leader of the Pack* in 1964. The song was written by George 'Shadow' Morton. Billy Joel played piano on Morton's demo track.

The track was recorded at the Ultrasonic Sound studio, which was located on the second floor of a Manhattan hotel. According to music legend, the revving motorcycle that can be heard in the recording was a real bike that they brought up to the studio in the hotel elevator.

Leader of the Pack hit #1 on the Billboard chart. It was refused airplay on the BBC (either because of the song's morbid theme, or possibly because it was felt that playing the song would encourage violence between the 'Mods' and the 'Rockers'.)

Rolling Stone rated it one of the 500 Greatest Songs of All Time. The song was also recorded by Twisted Sister, which gives it another motorcycle connection courtesy of Dee Snider.

Day 238 – **Motorcycle Mamas — both of 'em**

'Motorcycle Mama' was both a song and album title for Sailcat. If you don't remember the band, you're forgiven; they recorded one album only, in 1972. But the song is catchy as hell, with a lyrical hook that goes, "You'll be the queen of the highway, my motorcycle mama, and we'll see the world from my Harley".

Sailcat's *Motorcycle Mama* was a 'concept album', loosely structured around a hero's motorcycle journey. It even featured a groovy cover illustration of a sidecar rig.

A few years later, Rolling Stone called Neil Young's 1978 hit *'Motorcycle Mama'* "the most amiable heroin tune ever done." Indeed, the song's connection to motorcycles is tenuous, in spite of the title. I presume that at one time, Neil's supplier was a woman who rode a motorcycle.

It makes the list though, because Neil is an avid motorcyclist. In fact, years later he released another great motorcycle song, *'Unknown Legend'* about his wife Pegi, who also rode a Harley-Davidson.

Day 239 – *Little Honda*, by the Beach Boys and the Hondells

'Little Honda' was written by Brian Wilson and Mike Love. It's known to rock historians for its early use of guitar 'fuzz'.

The Beach Boys recorded it in the spring and released in the summer of 1964 on the album All Summer Long. As it happened, the record's release coincided with a major TV ad campaign by Honda— "You meet the nicest people on a Honda".

The song might as well have been an ad for Honda.

I'm gonna wake you up early 'cause I'm gonna take a ride with you
We're goin' down to the Honda shop, I'll tell you what we're gonna do
Put on a ragged sweatshirt, I'll take you anywhere you want me to

First gear, it's all right
Second gear, I'll lean right
Third gear, hang on tight
Faster, it's all right

It's not a big motorcycle, just a groovy little motorbike
It's more fun than a barrel of monkeys, that two-wheel ride
We'll ride on out of the town to anyplace I know you like

[Chorus]

It climbs the hills like a Matchless 'cause my Honda's built really light
When I go into the turn, lean with me, and hang on tight

*I better turn on the lights, so we can ride my Honda
tonight*

[Chorus repeats]

Honda must've been delighted, but things got even better
for Big Red when the song inspired Gary Usher, an L.A.
record producer. Usher teamed up with a local DJ to write
an entire album's worth of songs, which he recorded with a
group of talented session musicians including Glen
Campbell.

Usher then manufactured a boy band—The Hondells—to
tour and perform those songs. A few months later, The
Hondells released an eponymous album filled with still
more motorcycle songs.

'The Hondells' cover shows four guys in matching
sweaters standing around a Honda CL72 scrambler. The
songs included *'Black Denim'*, *'Lay it Down'*, and *'You're
Gonna' Ride With Me'*. A year later, the band appeared as
themselves in the movie *Beach Blanket Bingo*. The band
was active until 1970.

Day 240 – **Off the list: David Allan Coe's *Panheads
Forever***

Harley-Davidson got some *'Little Honda'* style love in the
David Allan Coe song *'Panheads Forever'*. The ballad
includes the line, "She knows when to run, and she don't
run around," and is, all in all, a fairly moving love song,
written about a motorcycle.

Coe also wrote *"Take This Job and Shove It"*, which
became a country anthem for Johnny Paycheck, so I want

to like him, in spite of his obvious anger issues. (He was known to ride his Harley onto the stage and scream insults at his audience.)

Unfortunately, I can't get past the fact that his album 'D.A.C. 18 X-Rated Hits' includes a song with this poetic line: "And then that scumbag mother fucker ran off with a nigger".

Day 241 – **Love and Rockets: *Motorcycle***

This is another love song to a motorcycle (refrain: "She's not gonna' let me down") written by Daniel Ash in 1988 and recorded by Ash's band Love and Rockets.

In spite of Ash's goth look and metal sound, he comes across as a far nicer guy than Coe, and Ash's love of motorcycles really does run deep. He first stole his dad's scooter at the age of 12. He's owned dozens of Harleys and Triumphs, and still rides between gigs (he's also a DJ), taking winding routes wherever there's a more interesting road.

He once crowd-sourced a recording project, offering one fan the opportunity to go on a motorcycle ride with him, and keep one of his Harleys—a bike Ash'd put 130,000 miles on.

Day 242 – **Arlo Guthrie's *The Motorcycle Song***

Arlo Guthrie was born to be a folkie; his dad was the iconic leftie troubadour Woody Guthrie. He became famous in his own right in 1967 with the release of an album called 'Alice's Restaurant'. That was also the title of a nearly 20 minute-long 'talking blues' song that filled the entire 'A' side of the album. Two of the tracks on the 'B' side were about motorcycling: 'The Motorcycle Song' and 'Highway in the Wind'.

The prevalence of motorcycle imagery in Arlo's music reflects the fact that he's been a lifelong biker. He's performed *The Motorcycle Song* in almost every concert he's ever given, and over the years it's grown into an epic (and funny) 'talking blues' monologue.

Interesting Fact: Guthrie's album title was inspired by a real restaurant, owned by his friends Alice and Ray Brock, in Stockbridge, Massachusetts. Not long after the record came out, a totally different Alice — Alice Taylor — bought a restaurant on Skyline Boulevard in Woodside, California. Ms. Taylor was tickled by the idea of naming it after the famous song.

I'm not sure whether Arlo Guthrie's ever stopped by the west coast 'Alice's', but since it's at the intersection of two great riding roads (CA 35 & 84) it's become a gathering spot for hundreds of motorcyclists every weekend.

Day 243 – *Beer, Gas, Ride Forever* by John Doe

John 'Doe' Duchac was one of the founders of the critically acclaimed L.A. punk band 'X'. He's also an actor; he starred in the weirdly compelling biker movie *'Roadside Prophets'* and composed the song *'Beer, Gas, Ride Forever'* that runs under the film's opening credits. He also released the song on his album *'Kissingsohard'*.

The record was not a commercial hit, but it earned a positive review by music-industry influencer Jason Roth, who wrote, "Though X has consistently flirted with rockabilly, Doe's two solo outings have consummated the attraction. The country sensibilities of *'Kissingsohard'* are conveyed not so much musically as they are through Doe's world-weary, darkly soulful vocals and his use of the paperback poetics that made X bards for the pogo set."

'Beer, Gas, Ride Forever' sits pretty much right in between punk, rockabilly, and outlaw country. But hey, on a motorcycle, you can ride between all those places.

Day 244 – **Twisted Sister's *Ride to Live, Live to Ride***

Twisted Sister went through so many personnel changes in its early years that they probably should've installed a revolving door in their dressing room. However, Dee Snider's been in the lineup since 1976. (With a break, presumably, to appear on 'Celebrity Apprentice' and 'Celebrity Wife Swap'.)

Dee's an avid biker. He wrote *'Ride to Live, Live to Ride'*, and it was pressed on *'You Can't Stop Rock 'n' Roll'* in 1983. Although it was never released as a single, *Ride to Live* includes the memorable couplet, "Have a drink of some Coke, gasoline or some rope". The song immediately entered heavy rotation in the band's live performances.

Dee's never stopped riding, either. The annual 'Dee Snider's Ride' is a charity fundraiser in support of the Harry Chapin Food Bank on Long Island.

Day 245 – *Midnight Rider*, by the Allman Brothers Band

Gregg Allman wrote most of the songs for the band's second album while living in a remote cabin outside

Macon, Georgia. (He liked working in the woods, where he could smoke pot without worrying about getting busted.)

'Midnight Rider' was released as a single in 1971. Although it was not an immediate chart-topper—perhaps because it did not fit neatly into a 'country' or 'Southern rock' genre—it was widely admired by other musicians. It's been covered by artists as varied as Joe Cocker and Willie Nelson. There was even a reggae version by Paul Davidson.

Gregg and his brother Duane were probably destined to love bikes, since they attended high school in Daytona in the 1960s. Considering that Gregg rode throughout the period in which he had a severe drug and alcohol problem, it's probably lucky he didn't kill himself, like his bro.

Still, he seems to have come out the other side of those issues; he's still performing and relatively healthy, and rides a sweet custom-painted Street Glide.

Gregg Allman has said *Midnight Rider* is the song he's proudest of in his entire career.

Day 246 – *Ballad of Easy Rider*

Peter Fonda originally wanted to use Bob Dylan's *'It's Alright Ma (I'm Only Bleeding)'* under the opening credits for *'Easy Rider'*. When he was unable to negotiate the rights to Dylan's performance, he then tried to get Roger McGuinn of The Byrds to record a cover version.

To cover his bases, Fonda also asked Dylan to write a new song. Dylan grabbed a napkin and scribbled, "The river flows, it flows to the sea/Wherever that river goes, that's where I want to be/Flow, river, flow". Then the singer told Fonda, "Give this to McGuinn. He'll know what to do with it."

McGuinn did know what to do with it. He wrote an elegiac ballad that—even though it includes no motorcycle imagery — nicely captures the sense of a ride, while it also foreshadows the film's darker themes.

Fonda screened the film for Bob Dylan. When the troubadour saw his name in the credits (as the co-author of the title song) he insisted that it be removed. McGuinn later said that Dylan didn't like the film. It's also possible that he felt he was being used to promote it.

The influential rock critic David Fricke said the song perfectly captured the social mood of late 1969 and highlighted "the weary blues and dashed expectations of a decade's worth of social insurrection."

Day 247 – *Born to be Wild*

Of course, the song most associated with Easy Rider is *'Born To Be Wild'*, by Steppenwolf. Rolling Stone magazine rated it #129 on its '500 Greatest Songs of All Time' list.

Considering that it's been hummed by generations of motorcyclists, it's perhaps ironic that the songwriter was not a rider. Mars Bonfire was a Canadian; the name on his birth certificate was Dennis Eugene McCrohan but he was also sometimes known as Dennis Edmonton.

Mr. Bonfire was inspired to write the song when he saw a poster advertising a motorcycle in a Hollywood shop window. He originally wrote the song as a ballad, and offered it first to a psychedelic rock band called 'The Human Expression'. When they passed on it, he brought it to Steppenwolf; his brother was the band's drummer.

Steppenwolf turned it into the first 'heavy metal' rock song. (Bonfire's "heavy metal thunder" lyric was the first use of the term in music.) The song had just come out when Hopper and Fonda were finishing up Easy Rider, and they first used it as 'place-holder' music during the editing process. Luckily, they decided to leave it in there. The song's been covered by everyone from Etta James to Blue Öyster Cult.

Day 248 – **The best motorcycle song of all time…**

… is *1952 Vincent Black Lightning* by Richard Thompson

You might be forgiven for asking, "Richard who?" because there are a lot more famous performers and songwriters on this list. But Richard Thompson, a musician's musician, has written the best song about the best motorcycle.

Thompson was casting about for song ideas, looking for English themes that were romantic without being corny. He settled on the Vincent Black Lightning motorcycle because, as he put it, "When I was a kid, that was always the exotic bike, that was always the one, the one that you went 'ooh, wow'." The song was released on his album *'Rumor and Sigh'* in 1991.

In 2011, Time magazine included *1952 Vincent Black Lightning* in 'All Time 100 Songs'—a list of "the most extraordinary English-language popular recordings since the beginning of Time magazine in 1923."

Bob Dylan has performed it in concert. It's also a favorite of Julia Haltigan, a New York based singer and all-around bombshell, who rides a 1970 Bonneville herself.

Haltigan loves the song because, as she says, "It's a perfectly written tragic love story that brings chills down your spine. I've literally been brought to tears while singing this song, as though the tragic events and moving sentiment were happening to me. He's a rebel who robbed his way to owning one of the most beautiful motorcycles, and when his lifestyle finally gets the best of him, he gives her the bike as a token of their young undying love. I mean to me that's right up there with 'Romeo and Juliet'."

"In fact," she adds. "As a biker myself, I think I'd appreciate that gesture more!"

•

Day 249 – **Worth Knowing: Cannonball Baker**

Erwin 'Cannonball' Baker was probably the best-known American motorcyclist during the first half of the 20th century. Although he got his start as a racer, he became famous for elaborately staged and carefully documented endurance records. He was into selfies before 'selfies' were even a thing, and he had a real knack for self-promotion; all in all, he probably should've been born in 1982 instead of 1882!

Baker won the first race ever held at 'the brickyard' in Indianapolis on an Indian. When he wasn't racing in organized events he raced trains from town to town. George Hendee, the founder of Indian, took notice and sent Baker on a well-publicized tour of Latin America in 1912. In 1914, he set the first of several coast-to-coast records.

Those early records were set at relatively low average speeds. It took Baker 11½ days to get from Santa Monica to Savannah – but considering the 'roads' of the day and the primitive suspension on his Indian, that was grueling. After setting dozens of U.S. records including many coast-to-coast and 'three flags' trips, he shifted his emphasis to automobiles in the 1930s.

Cool fact: Baker was also the first national commissioner for Nascar.

Day 250 – **Rotary Club International**

Felix Wankel was raised by a single mom, and couldn't afford to attend university, so he trained in the printing business (he lived in the Heidelberg region in Germany, where the manufacture of printing presses was a major industry.)

Wankel had always been fascinated by motorcycles and internal combustion engines, and one day when he was 17 he woke up having dreamt of "a new type of engine, half turbine, half reciprocating". He perfected his idea until he was almost 30, while contriving to receive unemployment benefits the whole time.

He and his mother were devoted Nazis, and Felix was the equivalent of a Scout Leader, except his Scouts were fresh-faced members of the Hitler Youth.

Wankel became a protégé of Robert Heinrich Wagner, who was an early and influential member of the German National Socialist Democratic Party. Those two had a falling out over a disagreement in the party direction; Wagner thought it should remain a political organization, while Wankel thought it should emphasize the paramilitary aspect. Wagner won out, at least temporarily, and had Wankel arrested.

Eventually, Wankel was freed by other Nazis who realized that his technical skills could help the German war effort. He was an SS officer for two years at the beginning of the war.

Wankel was briefly interned in the French sector after Germany's capitulation. But by 1951 he was back doing development work on his engine, with funding and assistance from NSU (a car company). Wankel and NSU demonstrated it to the German press for the first time in 1960.

Although he loved motorbikes as a kid, and sometimes worked under the table in a motorcycle shop while he was collecting the dole, he never rode or even had a driving license because his vision was not good enough to meet strict German standards.

Wankel sold his share of license royalties for his invention for 50 million Deutschmarks in 1971—about fifteen million bucks. The ex-Nazi became an ardent supporter of animal rights in later life.

His engine is, in theory, even more suited to motorcycles than cars. The design is compact, and it's possible to engineer a version that produces about 1 horsepower per pound of weight.

But, it's not without concomitant disadvantages; it's hard to seal the rotor, there are metallurgical challenges, and it's harder to make this type of motor meet modern emissions controls. Wankel motors also typically get poor fuel mileage, which is a bigger issue for motorcycles than cars.

In spite of those challenges, there have probably been more Wankel-engined motorcycles than you realize. Here are a few examples of the way this technology's been applied to bikes…

Day 251 – **MZ prototypes**

Motorrad Zschopau, in East Germany, was the first company to license Wankel's design from NSU, in 1960. At the time, MZ was dominating the world of high-output, small-displacement two-strokes, so they weren't looking at the Wankel as a race platform. Rather, the company thought the motors might be a superior alternative to the crude two-stroke motors that powered commuter motorcycles and the Trabant automobile.

MZ built at least two different Wankel-engined prototypes, one water- and the other air-cooled. The company seems to have had all the usual problems with apex seals, exacerbated by shoddy East Bloc metallurgy.

The Commies stuck by the terms of their development agreement, which lapsed at the end of 1969. At that point, all research and development on the Wankels came to a stop. So, although MZ was the first company to build a rotary-powered motorcycle, it never commercialized one.

Day 252 – **Hercules**

Fitchel & Sachs was a venerable German company that introduced the first bicycle freewheel. From 1929 onward, the company marketed Sachs two-stroke motors for motorcycles, chainsaws, generators, and anything else that needed a small, lightweight power plant. In the mid- '60s the company took over a series of struggling German motorcycle makers, including DKW and Hercules.

Fitchel & Sachs was the next company to license the Wankel engine for motorcycle use. The company showed a prototype Hercules road bike at a trade show in 1970.

The terms of the license were such that if the power output was greater than 30 hp, licensees had to pay higher royalties to NSU. The Hercules W-2000 was thus kept just below 30 hp. It was finally offered for sale in 1974.

In the United Kingdom, another company had the 'Hercules' trademark, so it was marketed in the U.K. as a DKW.

The marketplace consensus was that the machine was expensive and relatively underpowered. In spite of that, Fitchel & Sachs sold about 1,800 of them between 1974 and '79, and even produced an enduro version.

Around 1980, they sold their tooling to Norton.

Day 253 – **Suzuki RE5**

Suzuki began developing their Wankel project at around the same time as Fitchel & Sachs. Suzuki devoted a lot of effort to the surface of the trochoid block (aka 'cylinder' or combustion chamber) and filed a number of patents for metal treatments.

The RE-5 was intended to be Suzuki's flagship model. They hired Giorgietto Giugiaro to style the machine, and he delivered a motorcycle that had a distinctly space-age look. So much so that Suzuki hired an ex-Apollo astronaut, Edgar Mitchell, as a model spokesman.

You might guess from that, that Suzuki took the launch of this model incredibly seriously. They invited journalists to a week-long initial test, and promised buyers that if they experienced any motor problems in the first year, the entire power plant would be replaced.

The initial response was positive. American motorcycle magazines liked the bike's handling, and it produced decent torque. But, it was not as powerful as the GT-750 triple and worse, consumers rejected the styling. Suzuki immediately went back to the drawing board and produced a version with lights and instruments more like the GT's. It was too little, too late and the model was killed after only two years; Suzuki wrote off the tremendous development costs.

In 1985, Cycle World called it one the "Ten Worst Motorcycles", which was probably a tad harsh. If anything, Suzuki was guilty of trying too hard; the motorcycle was ingenious in some ways (a secondary set of points and spark plug cleaned up engine operation during deceleration) but it was hellishly complex in other ways (it had one carburetor but five throttle cables.)

Day 254 – **The early road-going Nortons**

Over the course of the 1970s, BSA, Triumph, and Norton were all merged under a much larger industrial conglomerate, Manganese Bronze Holdings. All the British brands fared increasingly poorly vs. Japanese competition, and both BSA and Triumph at least considered (and prototyped) Wankel engined motorcycles in a sort of last-ditch defense against the Jap invasion.

Around 1978, the parent company's Chairman, Dennis Poore, felt that the only way out for Norton was to refocus the brand, using Wankel engines (and applying whatever BSA and Triumph had learned) in a new and expensive line of premium motorcycles.

The first effort was deemed a failure and hidden away. Then, between 1984-'89, Norton sold about 500 P41 Interpol II rotary powered police motorcycles.

In the late '80s, Norton changed hands yet again and the new owner created the P43 Classic model by removing the fairing and luggage from the police bike. Although only 100 or so were sold, the Classic was in many ways a great machine.

Norton then created the water-cooled P52 Commander police bike, and a companion P53 civilian model. The production run only about 300 bikes.

Day 255 – **The 'John Player' RCW588**

A Norton employee, Brian Crighton, realized the air-cooled Wankel engine in those mundane police bikes could develop a lot more power. He fit his tuned 588cc motor into a Spondon beam chassis, and got Norton's attention and a lot more funding when his little team won the British F1 championship in 1987.

Norton continued to develop the RCW588 for several years, with some really notable successes: In 1992, Steve Hislop won the Senior TT in a duel with Carl Fogarty. Many people feel that it was the greatest single TT race. And in '94, Ian Simpson won the British Superbike Championship on the machine.

One of the last Norton rotaries was the 95 horsepower P55 F1, which was intended to be a top of the line sport bike. It too was built on a Spondon frame and it was expensive: £12,000 in 1990, or roughly $33,000 in today's terms. It had some issues, notably that heat built up inside its full bodywork.

Just before Norton went bust (for about the fourth- or fifth-last time) the factory built 66 road-legal replicas of the race bike out of spare parts. The P55B model, aka 'F1 Sport' had bodywork that allowed heat out. It remains the most sought after modern Norton.

All told, Norton probably built fewer than 1,000 rotaries. But they are still a fascinating study in what-might-have-been. Dennis Poore may have been right; maybe Norton really could have rebuilt its brand on the strength of those Wankels.

Day 256 – Van Veen OCR

The Norton P55B may have been the best of the road-going rotaries. But real Wankel fetishists will always put an asterisk on the Van Veen OCR; now *that* was a motorcycle that might have achieved greatness.

Hendrik 'Henk' Van Veen was known in the Grand Prix world as a great tiddler tuner; he built some of the fastest Kreidler 50cc Grand Prix bikes. (There was a 1/20th liter class in the World Championship from 1962-'83.) He was also the Kreidler distributor in Holland.

In the early '70s, Van Veen thought that the compact and powerful motors in some Mazda cars could, potentially, power a superbike. His first proof of concept was a Mazda motor in a Moto Guzzi chassis. It worked well enough to encourage him, but the big breakthrough came in 1973, when NSU and Citroen showed of the twin-rotor 'Comotor' Wankel engine that would power the new Citroen GS car.

The motor weighed a couple of hundred pounds, and generated more than 100 horsepower as well as over 100 pound-feet of torque. Van Veen arranged to buy motors from the NSU-Citroen venture, and contracted with Porsche for the design of the gearbox. The rest of the motorcycle was designed by an ex-racer named Jos Schurgers, who created a strikingly modern and handsome bike.

The Van Veen was the star of the Cologne Motor Show in 1974. It even eclipsed the new Honda Gold Wing. It featured cast wheels and twin hydraulic disc brakes up front (which were probably needed to haul the 650-pound beast to a stop.) In spite of its weight, it was one of the better handling and fastest bikes of its time.

Van Veen didn't manage to begin production for another few years, by which time Citroen had already given up on the Comotor. (In fact, Citroen chose to buy back the few hundred GS cars it had sold. They were all crushed so that the French company could avoid the expense of supplying parts and warranty service.)

The bike was priced at $15,000 in the late '70s. That was twice the price of the best BMWs at the time, and over $40,000 in today's terms. In spite of that, Van Veen sold almost 40 of them. The Van Veen story has a unique coda: Just a few years ago, someone bought all the tooling and spare parts, and built 10 more Van Veen rotaries on Niko Bakker frames. They were priced at an eye-popping $115,000 a piece.

Day 257 – **Yamaha, Honda, and Kawasaki prototypes**

All the other big Japanese manufacturers have, at one time or another, tested Wankel powered motorcycles. Yamaha was the first to do so, and the tuning forkers showed a water-cooled twin-rotor concept at the 1972 Tokyo Motor Show. They called it the RZ201. The bike looked quite finished, although Wankel experts point out that the single-layer exhaust header couldn't possibly handle the motor's intense exhaust temperatures in real-world riding.

Kawasaki took out a development license in 1971, and developed a twin-rotor, water-cooled motor that developed 85 hp. Judging from surviving photos, they tested a working prototype in the mid- '70s, on what looks like a KZ650 rolling chassis.

Although I've read that Honda never took out a development license, Honda definitely did build a single-rotor, air-cooled Wankel motor. Honda presumably considered it for use on a small commuter bike. (The company used an early '70s CB125 chassis as a test mule.)

In the end, it was never quite the right time for Wankel's invention. It took decades of development for rotor design and metallurgy to overcome wear at the various seals between the rotor and combustion chamber. By the time licensees had worked those bugs out, rising fuel prices and stricter emissions controls presented additional challenges.

Maybe Yamaha, Honda, and Kawasaki realized that the world was changing in ways that made Wankels less attractive. Or maybe they looked at Suzuki's RE-5 fiasco and just thought, "Phew! Better them than us."

Day 258 – Why be a Wankel when you could get blown?

Motorcycle designers flirted with Wankel motors because motorcycles obviously put a premium on motors that are powerful yet small and light. Of course, you don't have to get rid of pistons altogether; you can achieve big power gains with minimal additional weight, by adding a forced-induction system. (No I don't mean instituting a military draft; this is a different kind of forced induction.)

Forced induction is any means of compressing the air charge before it enters the intake port(s). Thanks to a bunch of science first described by guys like Antoine-Laurent de Lavoisier (science that, if you've been reading this book from front to back, you should know by now) the more oxygen molecules you can squeeze in there, the more gasoline you can mix in and burn. Since our atmosphere is easily compressed, a supercharged (or turbocharged) motor can produce a lot more power—easily enough to justify the relatively small additional weight of the blower.

A few years ago, the motorcycle world went into a delirious tizzy over the supercharged Kawasaki H2 and its even more ridiculous track-only variant, the H2R. They were described as the first supercharged production motorcycles, although of course they weren't the first motorcycles ever outfitted with superchargers.

Before WWII, there were several famous Grand Prix racers fitted with superchargers. And, in the 1980s quite a few big manufacturers experimented with turbocharging. What follows is a selective history of motorcycles with forced induction.

Day 259 – **Supercharging vs. Turbocharging**

Both systems use a spinning turbine or pump to compress the air-fuel mixture before it enters the combustion chamber. The difference is that a supercharger is mechanically driven (usually right off the crankshaft) while a turbocharger is powered by exhaust waste gases.

That means that the supercharger's drive mechanism costs power that would otherwise be available to spin your rear wheel, while the

turbocharger generates almost 'free horsepower'. That would seem to make turbocharging a more elegant solution, from an engineer's perspective.

The downsides to turbocharging are that the systems typically don't work well at low rpm, resulting in 'turbo lag'. That less of a problem in cars, which explains why quite a few cars have turbos, but only a few motorcycles.

Turbo systems also get extremely hot, and they have a tendency to heat the intake charge which causes it to expand (again with the science!). That's counter-productive so engineers typically want an intercooler to cool the intake air back down. It's easier to find space for an intercooler in a car than it is on a motorcycle.

The ability to design a supercharger that works over a wide rev range and didn't necessitate a second cooling system was enough for Kawasaki's engineers. Here are some other facts related to super- or turbocharged bikes.

Day 260 – **BMW's Kompressors — Amongst the first and now, most valuable!**

BMW began experimenting with superchargers in the mid-1920s. While the company's first 'Kompressors' weren't that successful in road racing, they made lots of power. By 1929, a 750cc Kompressor was the world's fastest motorcycle (ridden by Ernst Henne.) Supercharged BMWs held the outright motorcycle land speed record for the next ten years.

Throughout the 1930s, BMW refined their 500cc Grand Prix road racers. By 1935, the Type 255 'works' bikes had the supercharger at the front of the motor, and bevel-driven double-overhead cams. By '38, they'd incorporated a modern-looking hydraulic front fork and plunger rear suspension, giving riders a chassis that was nearly capable of handling the motor's power. And the last key to making the machines competitive was the liberal use of magnesium, keeping weight to around 300 pounds.

The apogee of the Type 255 came in 1939, when Georg Meier used one to win the Senior TT on the Isle of Man. Although the factory did not retain detailed records of which frames and motors won specific races, a '39 Type 255 similar to Meier's (if not that very one) sold for nearly half a million dollars at Bonham's 2013 auction in Las Vegas.

Day 261 – Gilera's Rondine

In the 1930s, almost every works racing team experimented with supercharging. BMW's Kompressors are now the best-known examples, but Gilera's 'Rondine' is perhaps even more legendary and was definitely more influential; it is the motorcycle that established the across-the-frame four-cylinder pattern that is still used for most sports bikes.

'Rondine' is the Italian word for 'swallow' — a swift bird. The Gilera Rondine began life in the 1920s as a project of two engineers, Carlo Gianni and Piero Remor, with the financial backing of the wealthy Count Bonmartini. The motorcycle racing project was eventually transferred to the C.N.A. aircraft company, and then sold again to Giuseppe Gilera in 1936.

In the last few years before WWII, the (now-Gilera) Rondine was probably the most powerful and technologically advanced 500cc Grand Prix racer. It was water-cooled, and had dual overhead cams. The Rondine's lay-down transverse four layout presaged the Yamaha FZ750's design!

The most striking feature of the pre-war Rondines was the 'Roots' blower that allowed it to produce about 80 horsepower, good for about 140 miles an hour. Dorino Serafini won the 1939 European 500cc Championship on it. Considering the tires, suspension, and brakes of the day, Serafini probably swallowed hard before races!

Day 262 – **The roots of 'Roots'**

A lot of Superchargers are 'Roots'-type blowers. You may not know that Roots blowers predate almost all internal combustion motors. (In fact, if you did already know that, I suggest you write your own damn trivia book!)

In 1860, Philander and Francis Roots, of Connersville, Indiana weren't even trying to compress air at all. They were trying to invent a more efficient form of water wheel. But, in dry-testing their water wheel, one brother accidentally blew off the other brother's hat.

That would have been a novelty at best, but when the superintendent of a local iron foundry heard about it, he realized the brothers' pump could make blast furnaces burn a lot hotter. The Roots patented their design for an air mover that was used in blast furnaces and to pump fresh air into underground mines.

At a smaller scale, Roots blowers' first automotive application was in Mercedes 'Kompressor' automobiles in the 1920s.

Day 263 – **World's only blown scooter? Meet the Peugeot Jetforce**

While Kawasaki recently claimed that its H2 was the first supercharged production motorcycle, it was certainly not the first supercharged production two-wheeler, because the

French company Peugeot produced a 125cc supercharged scooter in 2003.

The Peugeot Jetforce 125 Compressor offered performance that was striking, considering its small displacement, although it was probably put on the market a little too early. The Jetforce Compressor was cut from the Peugeot line after a few years, but the company produced a second supercharged scooter, the 20-horsepower Satelis model, from 2006-'12.

The Satelis was highly rated as a fast, comfy commuter scoot. One criticism was, however, that the space occupied by the blower cut into the storage area under the seat.

Day 264 – **The 'TC' stood for 'totally crazy'**
(or maybe 'Totalitarian Californians)

It took a long time for any major motorcycle manufacturer to cozy up to the idea of turbocharging. Kawasaki was careful to keep potential liability at arm's length when it came to the 1978 Kawasaki Z1-R TC. This US-only model was expressly sold without any warranty (or, presumably, life insurance.)

In 1977, a stock Z1-R was good for sub-12 second quarter mile times, with trap speeds of 110+ mph. That was impressive, but Kawasaki's US managers saw the writing on the wall when Honda unveiled the CBX, which was an even better stoplight drag racer.

Enter Kawi exec Alan Masek. He started a company called Turbo Cycle Corp., and worked with American Turbo-Pak to design a turbo that would increase the Z1-R's power from around 70 to over 100 horsepower at the recommended 6 psi of boost pressure.

Even though the bikes were sold fully kitted at Kawasaki dealers, Kawasaki got around both warranty claims and the EPA by claiming that the ATP kit was an aftermarket product.

The Z1-R TC had pretty good manners until around 6,000 rpm when the turbo kicked in, at which point things got totally crazy in a hurry. They got even crazier if customers cranked up the boost. That was easy to do; all it took was a screwdriver. After two years on the market, the California Air Resources Board passed regulations preventing dealers from selling new motorcycles with non-homologated exhausts, which pretty much put Turbo Cycle Corp. out of business.

About 1,600 Z1-R TCs were sold, and they're now pretty collectible.

Day 265 – **Honda CX500 Turbo**

Honda displayed the CX500 Turbo at the 1980 Cologne International Motorcycle Show. The model didn't reach dealers for another couple of years, but it was still the first production turbo from a major manufacturer in 1982.

Honda outsourced the turbo for this bike from Ishikawajima Heavy Industries Co. Besides the IHI turbo, the bike also featured programmed electronic fuel injection, Pro-Link rear suspension and a trick fork intended to reduce dive under braking. It's baffling that all that technology was applied to a pushrod v-twin.

The base-model (conventionally-aspirated) CX500 was a simple, rugged commuter bike favored by motorcycle couriers. In 1982, Honda offered a 650cc version of the standard bike. The 650 had a stronger crank, which was adapted for use in the 500 turbo, which operated at a relatively high 19 psi of peak boost. That doubled the horsepower of the standard 500.

The added performance came with serious turbo-lag, making it more of a high-speed touring bike than the sports bike Honda had intended.

The next year, Honda released a 673cc turbo, nominally known as the 650T. That model addressed the turbo-lag with lower boost pressure and a higher compression ratio. Honda built less than 2,000 of them in total.

Day 266 – **Yamaha XJ650LJ Seca**

Yamaha also released a nicely-style 650 turbo in 1982. Theirs was the XJ650LJ Seca. It was in many ways a more conventional bike — with an across-the-frame four-cylinder motor fed by Mikuni carbs. Perhaps because Yamaha bit off less of an engineering challenge, this machine was better-reviewed than the CX500 Turbo. (Like the CX, this Seca had shaft-drive, which suggests Yamaha had envisioned it as a bike for high-mileage riders.)

Yamaha scored a marketing coup when they arranged for it to be James Bond's ride in the 1983 movie 'Never Say Never Again'.

Day 267 – **The best and last: Kawasaki GPz750 Turbo**

Kawasaki was the last of the big Japanese manufacturers to offer a turbo in the early- to mid- '80s. Kawasaki originally began developing a 650cc turbo, but during the model's evolution it grew to 750cc.

The GPz750 Turbo was sold as a 1984 and (slightly improved) '85 model. In order to get around import tariffs, bikes destined for the U.S. and Canadian markets were assembled in Kawasaki's Nebraska plant.

Although the Turbo bore a strong family resemblance to the conventionally aspirated GPz750, Kawasaki didn't just plumb a Hitachi turbocharger into the stock exhaust system — far from it. The Turbo got fuel injection, lower-compression pistons, and stronger gearbox internals; even the steering geometry was changed.

In 1984, its performance put it on a par with open-class bikes. Kawasaki advertised it as "the fastest production motorcycle". But, like all the turbos, it came and went quickly; 1985 was the last model year. One of the reasons: State Farm Insurance listed the GPz750 Turbo (along with the Honda and Suzuki turbos) on a 'blacklist' of bikes it refused to insure.

Day 268 – What? No Harleys on this list?

The arguments against turbos — and to a lesser extent, superchargers — are that they tend to steepen power curves, increase weight and complexity, and of course price. Part-throttle performance issues are a bigger deal for motorcycles than cars, because bikes are more sensitive to handling problems as riders get on the gas in mid-corner.

On the face of it, you'd think that of all motorcycle manufacturers, Harley-Davidson would be the one whose products lend themselves best to forced induction. Harley motors are relatively low-rpm, understressed lumps; the bikes are already heavy and expensive, so added weight or cost would barely be noticeable; and few Harley riders are aggressively ripping along winding canyon roads where turbo lag would be a problem.

All that explains why there are dozens of aftermarket kits allowing owners to turbocharge or supercharge both V-Rods and air-cooled hogs.

And yet, Harley-Davidson has never sold a motorcycle equipped with either a turbocharger or a supercharger — the company doesn't even have a turbo or supercharging kit available in its extensive Screamin' Eagle performance catalog.

I guess that proves that — as important as Screamin' Eagle is to H-D's profits — it's not as influential as the company's in-house council, aka the department known as Screamin' Legal™.

.

Day 269 – **Worth Knowing: Harley-Davidson & Porsche**

Porsche is of course best known as a car company. But the company has a long tradition of providing specialized engineering and consulting services to other companies – from auto makers to aviation. Since 1996, such consulting services have been carried out by a subsidiary called Porsche Engineering.

Harley-Davidson has had a long relationship with Porsche going back to at least the mid- '70s with the ill-fated Nova Project. That was a modular v-two-, four-, or even six-cylinder motor designed by Porsche. Harley spent millions on quite a few prototypes, before deciding it would be too expensive to manufacture.

Their best-known collaboration led to the V-Rod motor. After a long, frustrating time trying to make the VR1000 superbike competitive, Harley-Davidson killed its road-racing program in 2001. But in order to try to capture some value from the VR1000 fiasco, The Motor Company sent a VR1000 motor to Porsche – giving it the assignment of turning it into a viable street motor.

Porsche retained the 60° v-angle, but by the time it had finished creating the 'Revolution' motor, that was the only dimension it shared.

In the late '90s, Harley-Davidson entered into a joint venture agreement with Porsche, resulting in the creation of a separate entity (a manufacturer of motorcycle powertrain components) 51% owned by Harley-Davidson. According to SEC filings, Harley-Davidson later bought Porsche out.

•

Day 270 – **A web site worth knowing: The Vintagent**

thevintagent.blogspot.com bills itself as "The world's #1 vintage motorcycle site" and I have no reason to doubt that claim. It's the brainchild of Paul d'Orleans, who had this to say about it…

The Vintagent is the oldest of the 'old bike' blogs, passing the 10-year mark in October 2016. Not old enough to drink yet, but big enough to kick your shins. What began as an all-consuming hobby (it spat out one marriage) has become an actual career as a writer; for magazines (I'm now an editor for Cycle World, At Large, and 1903) and a few books (The Ride, Café Racers, and The Chopper: the Real Story).

Before I got paid for my thoughts, The Vintagent racked up over 800 articles on my favorite rabbit holes – art, politics, sex, technology, and history, as seen from the handlebars of a beautiful motorcycle.

I combine my bent as an artist and motorcycle book collector (3000+ in the library, and a long wall of old magazines) with a brain burdened by a shitload of useless facts - on just about everything. Thus my review of a 1928 Brough Superior SS80 might include a little Shakespeare, a kick in the shins to T.E. Lawrence (who loved Broughs) for screwing up the Middle East's borders with Churchill, and an attempt to explain why the SS80 is so astoundingly beautiful.

I do my level best not to be an overbearing prick, to only write about interesting stuff, and to never fall for cliché. The Vintagent remains a very personal project stemming from my excessive passion for motorcycles, and has led me around the world many times to meet interesting folks, do research and test rides, and attend cool events. By God, somebody had to do it.

•

Is two-wheel drive still crazy, after all these years?

These days, it seems that there are more all-wheel drive cars and truck on the road than old-fashioned front- or rear-drive vehicles. Over the years, many companies have experimented with drive systems that feed power to a motorcycle's front wheel too.

Day 271 – **Mototractor? Rock on!**

Anyone who read pulp magazines like Popular Science in the 1960s remembers ads for the two-wheel drive Rokon Trailbreaker. It looked like a typical minibike from that period, fitted with huge balloon tires.

The Rokon was invented by Charlie Fehn, but the manufacturing rights were bought and sold several times, so the machines were made in different places by different companies, and fitted with a number of different utility motors. Most of the time, Rokon was careful not to even call its product a motorcycle. The preferred term was 'Mototractor'.

Day 272 – **Those things would go anywhere. Except Vietnam**

One of the guys who acquired Rokon's manufacturing rights was J.B. Nethercutt, who owned the Merle Norman Cosmetics chain. If crude two-wheel drive trail bikes don't seem like a natural fit with Merle Norman, consider this: At the height of the Vietnam War, Nethercutt had two draft-age sons. By getting the U.S. Army to evaluate the Trailbreaker, Nethercutt was able to employ his sons as 'military contractors' – exempting them from the draft.

Rokon is still in business, producing bikes that are almost unchanged. Prices range from about $6,500-$8,500. For information visit www.rokon.com.

Day 273 – **Yamaha tries hydraulic drive**

About 40 years after Rokon appeared on the scene, both KTM and Yamaha experimented with systems that used small hydraulic motors in the front hub. While KTM never got past the prototype stage, Yamaha put the WR450 2-Trac into limited production in 2004.

Yamaha's system had been developed by Öhlins in Sweden – at that time it was a Yamaha subsidiary. They also developed a two-wheel drive R1 sport bike, which performed exceptionally well in the wet (no surprise there.)

The Swedish engineer who headed the street bike project for Öhlins later said that ordinary riders loved two-wheel drive. It didn't catch on because professional test riders didn't like it (except when it was raining.)

Only about 250 2-Trac off-road rally bikes were produced.

Day 274 – **Steve Christini won't give up**

The last man standing, when it comes to two-wheel drive, is Steve Christini.

Christini perfected a lightweight mechanical system that provided drive to a mountain bike's front wheel in 1995. Within a few years, he had a working prototype for motorcycles, too. At first, Christini sold kits that adapted existing motorcycles. While expert riders don't find Christini's bikes to be better than the best rear-wheel drive alternatives, novices are capable of handling far more challenging terrain on a two-wheel drive bike.

He sold the first 'Christini' complete motorcycle in 2007, and has since focused a lot of his attention on military sales. Christini has a range of civilian bikes for sale at around $9,000. Civilian preppers can also buy the Military Edition, which can be configured in numerous ways, at prices north of $15k.

For more info, visit www.christini.com.

The five most bike-crazy states. And the least...

According to the Motley Fool web site, most American states average about one motorcycle registration for every thirty to fifty residents, but there's a wide range, from a high of one motorcycle per 12 residents in the most bike-crazed state to a low of less than one motorcycle per 100 residents in the lowest.

The states where bikes are (per capita) most common might surprise you. For example, you might think that states where there's a long riding season would dominate, but they don't: Alaska has one motorcycle for every 23 residents, while California has only one bike for every 47!

Day 275 – **At #5: Wyoming**

Wyoming — where winters are as long as the yawning distances between cafes and bars — should be an unlikely motorcycle market, right? Wrong.

There are only about 30,000 bikes in the entire state of Wyoming, but considering its sparse population (a little more than half a million residents) that's enough to earn it a Top Five spot, with one bike per 19 residents. Maybe it's because it's next door to the #1 state for bike ownership.

For the record, there is one horse for every five residents of Wyoming. That's why there's a cowboy on the state's license plate, not a biker.

Day 276 – #4: Wisconsin

Wisconsin doesn't have a long riding season, either, but the only surprise is that it isn't even higher on the list. Milwaukee, as Harley-Davidson's home town, is predictably bike-mad. If you haven't been to the Harley-Davidson Museum you owe it to yourself to visit — even if you don't ride a hog.

The state is home to Road America, one of the U.S.' top race tracks. The nearby Siebken's Resort has probably been the scene of more drunken hijinks by motorcycle racers than any other single bar in the country.

If you're the kind of rider who is more inclined towards sweeping bends, Wisconsin's 250-mile Great River Road clings to the eastern bank of the Mississippi.

Day 277 – #3: Iowa

Wisconsin's neighbor Iowa also has about one bike per 18 residents. Now, most people probably don't immediately have motorcycles come to mind when they think 'Iowa'. (Most people never think 'Iowa' to begin with, except in years when it hosts an early Presidential Caucus.) But the state earns its motorcycle cred with a major assembly plant in Spirit Lake — that's where Polaris Industries makes Victory engines, and assembles Indian motorcycles.

The unlikely town of Anamosa — between Cedar Rapids and Dubuque, if that's any help — is also the home of the self-proclaimed National Motorcycle Museum, with over 400 historic motorcycles on display.

Day 278 – Live Free and Ride: New Hampshire

With one bike registered for every 17 residents, New Hampshire is the second most motorcycle obsessed state in the Union. It's also the home of one of the country's largest motorcycle gatherings.

Laconia Motorcycle Week dates back to 1916, when motorcyclists from across New England met up at Weirs Beach. For years, the week coincided with an AMA 'National' road race at the old Bryar Motorsport Park.

Motorcycle Week ran afoul of the law in 1965, when thousands of motorcyclists clashed with police, prompting the Governor to call out the National Guard. Like the famed Hollister 'riot', which happened in California about 20 years earlier, the Laconia incident was breathlessly reported; some papers claimed 10,000 bikers were involved, although the number of actual rioters was far smaller.

One difference between the two events was that Hollister was really just run-of-the-mill hooliganism, while there was a genuine riot at Weirs Beach, complete with overturned and burning cop cars, tear gas, and fixed bayonets (wielded by National Guardsmen, not bikers.)

Day 279 – **And the winner is: South Dakota**

The small town of Sturgis in South Dakota's scenic Black Hills hosts the world's biggest motorcycle rally. That probably helps to account for the fact that there's a motorcycle for every 12 residents in the state.

The town, with a permanent population of less than 7,000, claims that something like half a million bikers descend upon it for one week each August. (If those numbers seem unrealistic, it's because they're based on Dept. of Transportation automated traffic counters, and they likely count a lot of people who cross the counters several times during their stay.)

Whatever the real number is, the annual pilgrimage of hundreds of thousands of bikers has a huge economic impact for the entire state. And, when the Rally isn't on, the Black Hills are still terrific riding country.

Day 280 – **At #50: Mississippi**

I'd say, "last but not least, there's Mississippi" but it's both last and least. The most motophobic state in the Union.

Mississippi has just one registered bike per 112 residents, in spite of a year-round riding climate. The explanation is probably pretty simple: It's also the poorest state, by a fairly wide margin.

The state's low-lying terrain means that most of the roads are flat and straight. The web site MotorcycleRoads.com makes a few half-hearted suggestions for possible rides, but lists only one regularly occurring motorcycle gathering — an ABATE rally you should probably only attend if you have determined that the thing that's missing in your life is angry old white guys with beer bellies.

•

Pick just 10… Harley-Davidsons

When a company's been producing motorcycles for well over a century, it's hard to narrow a "dream garage" to just 10 bikes. To say nothing of Harley's bewildering nomenclature; is that an FXRS, or an FXDP?

In spite of those challenges, here's my 'Top Ten' hogs… with the proviso that I've limited this list to production bikes. I've left most factory race bikes off the list, along with priceless and unobtainable very early models.

Anyway, here's my choice of ten prize hogs…

Day 281 – Model 11F

In 1915, the introduction of the Model 11F took Harley's 'silent grey fellows' to a new level.

The 11F had a 61 cubic-inch, inlet-over-exhaust valve motor that made 11 horsepower. The motor itself had bigger bearings made in-house. It was mated to a three-speed transmission, and featured automatic oiling — riders of previous models had to pump oil from the oil tank into the top end of the motor by hand every few minutes.

Harley sold almost 10,000 of them, so it was a big commercial hit. In many ways it's the definitive pre-war hog, and by far the most robust and rideable of the early Harley-Davidsons. The 'J' model had electric (as opposed to acetylene) lights. The J's tail-light could even be removed to serve as a work light at night!

Day 282 – JDH 'Twin Cam'

After the First World War, Harley was ascendant while Indian was already in decline. However, sport-oriented riders still preferred the Indian 101 Scout, or Excelsior Super-X twins, or Henderson fours.

Harley needed a fast sport bike to round out its line. In the 1920s, Harley's factory race bikes featured twin cams (which reduced reciprocating mass in the valve train and allowed higher revs.) Those twin-cammers were unobtainable to the public until 1928, when the company released the JH (61 cu. in.) and JDH (74 cu. in.) models.

The JDH was one of the last Harleys sold with inlet-over-exhaust valves; the company was about to switch to more-reliable flathead motors. It would be some time before they sold another production bike as fast at the JDH.

In its day, the JDH was expensive — as much as a Model A Ford — so it was not a big seller. But, it's a reminder that Harley has produced real 'superbikes' over its history.

Day 283 – One of the first Knuckleheads: Harley EL

I have nothing against the flatheads of the '20s and '30s, but the next time Harley-Davidson produced a really state-of-art motorcycle was in 1936 with the release of the 61 cubic-inch overhead-valve E models.

The company officially called this new motor the OHV, but it came to be called the Knucklehead, because the rocker covers protecting the overhead valves looked like two knuckles. The valve-train wasn't the only improvement; it had a dry sump, a better clutch, and a four-speed tranny.

Harley offered three Knuckleheads in the mid- '30s: the 'E' model, with 37 horsepower; the 'ES', specifically prepped for sidecar work; and the 'EL' model — also called the 'Special Sport Solo' — with a higher compression ratio. The latter was by far the most popular, but at the height of the Depression sales were, well, depressed. As a result, they're rare now.

The bikes had swooping Art Deco-inspired lines. Combined with the brawny OHV motors, they set the pattern for present-day Harleys.

Day 284 – One of the first Panheads: '48 FL

In 1948, the company updated the big twins again. They got aluminum heads that provided better cooling. Again, the shape of the rocker covers quickly earned them a new nickname — 'Panheads'.

Panheads were sold in two displacements, E models with 61 cubic inches and F models with 74 cubic inches. There were three variants of each; a base model, a sidecar tug with lower gearing, and a Special Sport Solo version with higher compression. The sporty EL and FL ones sold the best.

Panhead motors remained in production until 1965, with incremental improvement. They remain the definitive 'chopper' motor. Perhaps that's why I'd specify a '48 in this case; that was the last year for springer forks.

Day 285 – **The '55 & '56 KHK**

After WWII, an influx of light and powerful 500cc overhead valve twins from Britain threatened Harley's dominance of the American market. In 1952, Milwaukee fired back with the 'K' model, which still had a flathead 750cc motor, but an upgraded chassis including rear shocks (six years before the Duo-Glide!) It also featured the foot shift and hand clutch arrangement found on the British bikes and preferred by racers.

The K was still underpowered, compared to higher revving British twins, so in 1954 Harley increased the displacement of the KH model to 883 cc. That was a cool enough bike for Elvis Presley, who bought one.

The final flowering of the flatheads was the KHK model, which produced more power thanks to a roller-bearing bottom end, bigger valves, and better porting. It was the closest street bike to the venerable KR racer, and the direct ancestor of the Sportster.

Day 286 – **The first of the Electra-Glides**

In 1965, Harley offered electric start for the first time on FL models. (Electric starters had been offered on Servi-Car trikes a few years earlier.

The '65 'Glide was the first year for electric start and the last year of the Panhead. In addition to a bigger battery and 12-volt electrical system, it also got a larger stock fuel tank.

I have to admit that, of the bikes in my personal dream garage, the first Electra-Glide is perhaps the least-defensible choice. It is in many ways pretty archaic. Harley actually still offered an optional hand-shift. The brakes were nowhere near as good as those on European bikes. And the first electric starter proved vulnerable to moisture and corrosion— which was ironic considering that it was a unit designed for use on *boats*.

Still, it was one of the better long-range tourers of its time, and the first bike with all the key elements of the present day Harley-Davidsons (including their weaknesses!) Interestingly, 1965 was also the first year Harley-Davidson was a publicly traded company.

Day 287 – **1982 FXR Super Glide II and FXRS**

Harley's first time as a publicly traded stock ended when the company was acquired by AMF in 1969. The AMF years are remembered less than fondly!

In 1981, "The Eagle Soared Alone" again after an employee-led buyout. The first new platform was the FXR. Freed from the shackles of AMF, Harley's design team set out to build a motorcycle that — while still a Harley — could really compete with the imports.

The FXR was the first Harley chassis influenced by road-racer and engineer Erik Buell. It was sold in two versions, the Super Glide II with spoked wheels and the FXRS with cast wheels. Both had 'Shovelhead' motors (though again, freed from AMF, quality improved.)

They were exceptionally good-handling bikes, with a stiff frame and ample cornering clearance. In spite of that — or perhaps because of that — they weren't great sellers. And, the models had some enemies within Harley-Davidson. It's said that styling chief Willie G. Davidson felt they looked "too Japanese". Nowadays, there are many Harley aficionados who say those early FXRs were the best Harleys ever.

Day 288 – **XR1000**

Just a year after the FXR, Harley took another shot across the bow of high-performance Japanese musclebikes with another short-lived/now-loved sport bike: the XR1000.

For years, Harley-Davidson execs and dealers had fantasized about selling an XR750 flat track bike for the street. Once Harley had committed to a new Sportster based on the XRX frame, Willie G. thought they could build a 1,000cc Sportster with XR750-style heads. That assignment went to Dick O'Brien, the legendary manager of Harley's race shop.

It turned out to be harder than it looked, but O'Brien (and more importantly, Harley's top execs) remained committed to the project. The result is basically an early '80s Sportster with the characteristic twin carb and twin forward-facing exhausts that define the XR750 flat track racer. How committed were they? Every top end was shipped to California where it was breathed on by Jerry Branch, then returned to Wisconsin for final assembly.

The XR1000 was delivered in a relatively mild state of tune, but there were performance parts available that could push output to nearly 100 horsepower. O'Brien immediately set to work fitting a tuned XR1000 mill into an XR750 chassis, and the resulting motorcycle — dubbed 'Lucifer's Hammer' — won the AMA's Battle of the Twins class.

Meanwhile, the stock bike — in best Harley fashion — had much to criticize. Although it would spin to well over 6,000 rpm, doing so threatened to shake your eyeballs out of their sockets. And the four-speed Sportster transmission was primitive. And then there was the price: Around $7,000 in 1983. Less than 2,000 were sold as '83 and '84 models, before Harley gave up on it. That explains why they're so sought after now.

Day 289 – 2001-'04 FXDP Dyna Defender

At the turn of the new millennium, Harley-Davidson was losing police fleet sales, as motorcycle cops preferred more maneuverable bikes like the BMW RT-P. And the Nebraska-built Kawasaki KZ1000 police model also gave police departments another made-in-the-USA option.

Harley responded by designing the FXDP Dyna Defender, which had a solo saddle, taller rear shocks, dual disc brakes up front, and stout hard boxes. Harley blacked out the motor to give it a suitably badass look, and the result was a good handling bike with clean, functional lines.

In spite of the low production numbers (around 1,200 in total) Harley couldn't sell them all to police departments, so quite a few ended up on dealer floors and subsequently in civilian hands. It's the closest thing you can ride to an archetypal cop bike, without being charged with impersonating a police officer.

Day 290 – The dragstrip-only VRXSE V-Rod Destroyer

The original V-Rod was introduced for the 2002 model year. The 1,130 cc 'Revolution' engine was another project in which Harley-Davidson sought the input of Porsche.

The goal was to build a bike for the sort of rider who might, otherwise, be drawn to a Yamaha V-max.

The V-Rod was radically different than any previous Harley; different enough that a lot of hard-core Harley fans didn't take to it. And, it largely failed to attract new customers (at least, in the U.S.) After a few years of lackluster sales, dealers told the company it had to do something to sex up the V-Rod's image. Dealers got what they asked for at the 2005 dealer presentation, in Las Vegas, when Harley unveiled a version that wasn't even street-legal: The V-Rod Destroyer.

The VRSXE featured a heavily breathed-on engine with a lightened stroker crank yielding a 1,300 cc displacement and ports so cavernous that they had to cast all-new heads to accommodate them. A special drag-racing clutch with a two-stage lockup helped transmit 165 hp and, more to the point, over 100 pound-feet of torque to the strip. A long wheelie bar gave it an, "Are you looking at me?" attitude. The price was just north of $30 grand.

At the meeting, Harley said that its Custom Vehicle Operations department would limit numbers to around 250. It must've been a hell of a presentation because dealers placed orders for over 600. Harley agreed to build and deliver that many, but after that early flush of enthusiasm, it turned out there were nowhere near 600 customers who actually wanted to become amateur drag racers.

Most sold to collectors — and I strongly suspect that dealers sold the last few at substantial discounts. Some people bought VRSXE models just to pull the motors and use them in other customs. But it remains by far the quickest and fastest stock Harley-Davidson — easily capable of sub-10-second quarters.

•

Day 291 – **Worth Knowing: Rollie Free**

Roland 'Rollie' Free set a famous land-speed record on the Bonneville Salt Flats in 1948, when he stripped down to a bathing suit and, lying prone on the back fender, broke the 150 mile-an-hour barrier on a Vincent.

Free was born in Chicago in 1900. He raced on board tracks and dirt tracks, until the Second World War. During the war, he worked in aircraft maintenance at Hill Field, in Utah. That may have been when he developed an interest in land-speed racing.

After the war, Vincent's Phil Irving was visiting the U.S. when he encountered John Edgar, a writer and sportsman, at a Burbank bike shop. Edgar convinced Irving that Harley-Davidson's existing land-speed record was within reach. Soon afterward, Irving supervised the modification of a Series B Black Shadow – work that effectively served as the prototype for the Black Lightning.

Edgar then hired Free to ride the bike. Free normally wore some protective clothing, but he'd seen another land-speed racer, Ed Kretz, strip down to reduce wind resistance.

•

What is that? Some kind of motorcycle?
Trikes and other oddities

Some of the very first 'motorcycles' were actually tricycles. In fact, if you could travel back in time and stand on the sidewalk of the Champs-Élysées in the late 1890s you'd find that trikes outnumbered both cars and bikes in those very early days of internal combustion.

Now, as the baby boomers age, three wheels are making a big comeback. Here's a bit of trike history, and some stories of other bikes that, over the years, have challenged motorcycle orthodoxy.

Day 292 – De Dion-Bouton scored the first big success

This French company was founded by the Marquis Jules-Albert de Dion, Georges Bouton, and Bouton's brother-in-law Charles Trépardoux in 1883. The trio were originally interested in creating steam-powered vehicles, and sold a number of steam powered tricycles. But, within a few years, they realized that internal combustion was where it was at.

At the end of the 19th century, De Dion-Bouton was the largest 'automobile' company in the world, although their best-selling product was a light tricycle.

Those early trikes had small, relatively high-revving motors producing from one to two horsepower. They were built on chassis supplied by another company, Decauville, and fitted with Michelin pneumatic tires. They were set up with a solo seat, but a 'carriage' trailer was available, allowing for passengers. De Dion-Bouton sold 15,000 trikes before shifting production exclusively to automobiles in 1901.

Day 293 – **The family that rides together…**

Although guys had been grafting auto rear ends (often Volkswagens) to chopper front ends throughout the '70s, the modern trike phenomenon dates to 1984.

That was when John Lehman of Westlock, Alberta set out to make a 'motorcycle' that his wife Linda would ride. (Presumably she refused to ride anything that threatened to just fall over by itself!)

Lehman grafted the rear axle of a Chevy Vega to a Honda CB900. It worked so well that he kept it for himself. Within a year, he'd built a trike (with a wooden body!) on a Gold Wing. Whenever he rode his trikes, people stopped him to ask about them and Lehman Industries was in the trike business in no time.

In 1990, Lehman took a GL1200 trike to Sturgis, and it won the Rat's Hole custom competition. A few years ago, he was inducted into the Sturgis Motorcycle Museum's Hall of Fame, where he is described as father of the modern trike.

Day 294 – **Harley tries its hand**

Harley-Davidson made the Servi-Car from 1932-'74, but it was only ever intended for slow-speed urban use. Still, Harley execs couldn't fail to notice the business done by trike conversion companies like Lehman — especially because in the early 2000s, the average age of a Harley buyer was increasing every year.

In 2008, Harley-Davidson entered into an agreement with Lehman, shipping Electra Glide Ultra Classic front halves to Lehman's plant in Spearfish, SD. From there, assembled trikes made their way into Harley dealerships as FLHTCUTG models. (I don't suppose they even bothered registering that as a trademark. Who else would want it?)

Besides the obvious rear axle, a few less-visible mods included a stronger 'police duty' clutch and triple clamps to revise rake and trail, reducing steering effort. An electric reverse gear was an $1,195 option; a handy one, considering that the Tri Glide weighed about 1,200 pounds.

Plenty of motorcyclists turn up their noses at trikes, but the Tri Glide has recently been the fourth-best-selling Harley, out of a lineup of over 30 models.

Day 295 – **Can-Am Spyder**

Bombardier Recreational Products was, until recently, better known as a maker of water vehicles — whether the water was frozen (Ski-Doo) or liquid (Sea-do).

The company was a big innovator in those categories, and it made a daring bet in the late '90s when it set out to redefine 'trike' by putting the two wheels up front. BRP spent a lot of time in the R&D and design phases, but the company kept its secrets well; it surprised the entire powersports world when it unveiled the Spyder in 2007.

The Spyder's only 'motorcycle-ish' component was the 990cc Rotax v-twin motor (which bore a fairly strong family resemblance to the motor supplied to Buell for the

1125.) The rest of it was kind of a mashup of a snowmobile chassis, with a car's modern traction control.

Although the Spyder has probably caused more people to ask, "Is that a motorcycle?" than any other vehicle, its three-wheeled architecture made it a motorcycle, at least from a legal perspective, in most jurisdictions. That meant that buyers had to have a motorcycle license. That must have hampered sales, but not much; in spite of launching right before the recession, Can-Am was completely taken aback by the demand for it. (I've heard that product planners set a goal of something like orders for 1,250 Spyders in the first year, and that they actually sold ten times that many.)

It's about 500 pounds lighter than a Harley-Davidson Tri Glide.

Day 296 – **Polaris Slingshot**

Judging from the seven-year gap between the first Can-Am Spyder and the first Slingshot, Polaris was caught on its back foot by the success of the new trikes. While Polaris says, "Slingshot is a three-wheeled motorcycle" on its web site, it's actually far more car-like than any other trike. The driver and passenger sit side-by-side, and the driver uses a steering wheel, not a handlebar.

From an American legal perspective, the big distinction between cars and motorcycles is not the number of wheels, but the fact that three-wheelers don't need to pass auto safety standards.

Depending on what state you're in (I'm referring to state as in 'California', 'New York', etc., not sober, drunk, or stoned) the Slingshot may be classified as a motorcycle, an auto-cycle, or a 'mototricycle'. Some states allow users to operate these vehicles with a simple driver's license, while others require a motorcycle endorsement. Most of the latter group allow you to take your motorcycle test on a trike.

The explosive growth of 'reverse trikes' like the Spyder and Slingshot mean give BRP and Polaris both the means and a strong motive to lobby for their continued status as some kind of 'motorcycle'.

That said, the Department of Transportation and the National Highway Transportation Safety Administration are currently considering the legal requirements for such vehicles. NHTSA has said, *"NHTSA believes consumers who purchase these vehicles are likely to assume that these vehicles have the same safety features and crash protection as passenger cars certified to Federal safety standards."*

Making trikes meet automotive safety standards would essentially kill the category. That puts BRP in Polaris in a tricky situation: They're busy lobbying states to argue that any car driver should be able to legally operate one, while they're lobbying the federal government to continue regulating them as motorcycles.

Day 297 – **Leaning towards being a scooter: Ariel 3 and Honda Gyro**

Cats hate the expression, "There's more than one way to skin a cat." But the remarkable diversity of trike designs suggests there are many ways to steer and power a three-wheeler. In 1969, one of BSA's last gasps was the 50cc

Ariel 3 scooter, which looked like the front end of a scooter grafted onto a large picnic cooler with wheels. It could be operated completely upright, like child's tricycle, at walking speeds, but it was articulated, leaning into turns like a scooter.

The Ariel 3 might have leaned in turns, but it flopped in the marketplace.

Although it was a commercial failure, the underlying patents were held by G.L. Wallis & Son, a small design firm in England. Once BSA had abandoned the project, Wallis approached all the big Japanese companies, and in the early '70s Honda, Suzuki, and Yamaha all sent engineers over to evaluate Wallis' ideas.

Honda was the next to license Wallis' patents and it produced the conceptually similar (but superior in every way) 'Stream' model in 1981. The Stream was intended as urban personal transport but only lasted a few years; it was too expensive when compared to the popular Honda Cub.

Honda then redesigned it as the 'Gyro'; a utilitarian micro-cargo vehicle. Variants of the Gyro are still in production and remain popular as delivery vehicles in Japan.

Day 298 – **Honda Neowing**

You've probably noticed that there are a number of popular trike conversions of the Honda Gold Wing. Honda has left that market to companies like Lehman, probably because of their once-burned-twice-shy experience with the ATC trike — a vehicle that prompted a Consumer Products Safety Commission ban in the '80s.

But if you wonder how long Honda will ignore the booming trike sector, you may find out soon. Honda's shown a vehicle it calls the NEOWING, which is proportioned like a Spyder but is designed to lean into turns. Honda's take on the category looks to combine the stability of the Slingshot with a much more 'motorcycle-like' riding experience.

The company's filed a raft of patents related to this suspension and layout, and people who've seen the show bike up close say that it looks production ready.

Day 299 – **Piaggio MP3 spawns imitators**

Honda's not nearly the first manufacturer to design a leaning three-wheeler. The first one that achieved good market (and traffic!) penetration was the Piaggio MP3, which is a three-wheeled maxi scooter with two closely spaced front wheels that both lean in turns. That front suspension arrangement is the key to Piaggio's design; it resembles an automotive independent front suspension.

The MP3 looks weird at first — and it's admittedly quite a lot heavier than a standard scooter — but two front wheels provides superior stability and confidence, especially on wet roads. Since it leans, the front wheel track can be kept narrow; it's as easy to filter between cars as it would be on a conventional motorcycle. The front wheels lock upright at walking speed, so there's no need for a kickstand (or slow-speed balancing skills.)

The MP3's a hit in Europe. It can be operated with an ordinary car license in many European countries.

They say imitation is the sincerest form of ~~flattery~~ plagiarism. Yamaha and Peugeot have both tried to horn in on Piaggio's threesome action, with scoots called the Tricity, and Metropolis. Piaggio sued them. (In Yamaha's defense, the Tricity used a visibly different front suspension system.)

Day 300 – **Peraves EcoMobile/Monotracer**

A Swiss pilot named Arnold Wagner designed a fully enclosed motorcycle in the early 1970s. Since it was far more aerodynamic than conventional bikes, his 'EcoMobile' got terrific fuel mileage.

Wagner's company, Peraves, has built and sold hundreds of his cycles, which feature a long wheelbase and a racecar-like seat and harness for the rider. Since you can't put your feet down, a set of training wheels pop out at low speed.

Most of the Peraves cycles sold have been powered by a version of the four cylinder BMW K100 motor. Although they make less than 100 horsepower, they're fast. Wagner says the sensation of operating one is the closest thing you can get to flying on the ground. It's safe to say that a few drivers on the Autobahn have probably thought they were being passed by a UFO.

The EcoMobile is a quality piece, with a beautiful Kevlar monocoque chassis. It's priced accordingly, from $80-100k depending on specification.

A few years ago, Peraves decided to switch to electric power, and the all electric Monotracer is even faster. A Monotracer shared the Automotive X-prize a few years ago, by getting the equivalent of 300 miles per gallon. The U.S. Secretary of Energy was on hand at the prize ceremony; he described the Monotracer as exactly the kind technology the world needed to fight global warming and break America's addition to fossil fuels.

Ironically, a couple of years later when Peraves attempted to ship one of the first production Monotracers to California, customs agents threatened to crush it because they couldn't assign it to any existing import category.

Day 301 – **Dan Gurney's Alligator**

Dan Gurney is an American auto racing legend. His All-American Racers company has designed and built sports cars, Champ (aka 'Indy') cars, and a race-winning Formula One car. But he's also a bike nut, with some very unique ideas about motorcycle design.

Since 1980, Gurney's been developing a motorcycle he calls the 'Alligator'. Considering his race car background, it's not surprising he favors a low center of gravity. That's why his 'Gator is long and low. The rider sits like a race car driver on a low seat just 18 inches from the ground. Everyone who's tried it comes back saying its like riding a cruiser with the performance envelope of a crotch rocket. (In spite of the fact that most of them have been built with relatively low-powered single-cylinder Honda motors.)

Gurney always said he was going to limit production to 36 vehicles, to commemorate the number 36 on his Eagle F1 car. The 'Gator carried a nominal price of $35,000, which was not that high considering the high spec of the machine — such as carbon-fiber bodywork and Dymag wheels.

Day 302 – **Too good not to make it into production: Gibbs Biski**

Alan Gibbs is an eccentric Kiwi (as in 'New Zealander'; he's not actually a flightless bird).

The serial entrepreneur developed an interest in amphibious vehicles in the early 1990s. Gibbs Sports Amphibians is a company with R & D and manufacturing operations in Nuneaton (England), Auckland (New Zealand) and Detroit. The company already markets one product, the Quadski, which it describes a 'personal sports amphibian'.

The Quadski is a powered by a 140 horsepower BMW motor (similar to the one in the K1300 sports-tourer) giving it a top speed of 45 miles an hour on either land or sea.

As cool as it is, it's nothing compared to the Biski — a concept vehicle that is currently in the advanced prototype stage and which will likely come to market.

The Biski is a 500-pound maxi scooter that looks like a distant cousin of a Yamaha T-Max, except that it's essentially instantly amphibious. It will go 80 miles an hour on land, and you can ride it straight into the water. Switching from conventional rear wheel power to 'jet ski' mode takes about five seconds, and it will go 30 miles an hour on the water. Total James Bond material!

No suggested pricing has been released, but the Biski should be cheaper than the Quadski, which sells for around $40,000.

Day 303 – **Too ambitious to make it into production? The Lit C-1**

If there's one high-tech oddball 'motorcycle' that everyone's seen — at least on the Internet — it's the Lit C-1.

Like a lot of San Francisco tech startups, Lit talks a great game and generates lots'o buzz. Its videos have been viewed millions of times on YouTube, despite the fact that they show only computer simulations and prototypes operating at walking speed. Lit's received a couple of million bucks from investors ranging from Mark Pincus (his gaming company, Zynga, made him a billionaire) and surf icon Kelly Slater.

The company's proposed C-1 is another fully-enclosed, electric 'cabin motorcycle' (it looks quite a bit like the Monotracer). The big difference is that the Lit doesn't need 'training wheels' at slow speed because it's gyro-stabilized.

Gyro-stabilizing a single-track vehicle seems like an intuitively good idea at first, because falling over is a drag (as we all know.) The challenge comes when you consider that at anything over walking speeds, motorcycles must lean to steer.

It might be relatively easy to design a system that used gyros to keep a single track vehicle upright at very low speed, and then cut the gyros out to balance conventionally at normal speeds. (It might be easy, but it wouldn't be any better than Peraves' low-speed stabilizers, or using a narrow dual-track system at one end, as Piaggio did.)

Anyway, Lit's not taking the easy road. The company says it will use gyros to control lean angles at all speeds, in all corners. That would make it the only single-track vehicle that could be steered conventionally, like a car — no countersteering required.

•

Day 304 – **Diesels!**

Back in the days of the 125 and 250GP classes, the riders of those tiny, perfect little two-stroke racing motorcycles used to refer to the four-stroke Supersport and Superbike classes as 'diesels'. They were using the term as an insult. But are they that bad? (Answer: Yeah, probably.)

Although the U.S. military has acquired a few diesel motorcycles from Hayes Diversified Technologies, the number of diesel motorcycles available to American civilians hovers around zero. That's not to say there isn't interest — or at least curiosity. If Hayes' diesel-converted KLR650 was ever made available to the public, I'm sure a few adventure bike extremists would want one.

In Europe, far higher fuel prices have resulted in an increased acceptance of diesel. There has long been a little 'community' of people who've converted motorcycles to diesel, using small diesel motors designed for farm or industrial applications. And in the last few years, upstart manufacturers have built motorcycles powered by motors originally intended for compact cars. At least one company's devised a very creative solution to certain small-diesel balance challenges. And diesel motorcycles are already a bit of a niche in India. So, maybe diesel won't be a slur forever.

Day 305 – **Sooraj**

Sooraj Automobiles Limited is an Indian company that makes utilitarian three-wheeled cargo and passenger vehicles. Decades ago, Sooraj offered a diesel conversion of the Royal Enfield Bullet. When those proved (surprisingly) popular, Sooraj made and sold their own 325cc diesel.

The single-cylinder motor produced only about 6.5 horsepower and, for a diesel it wasn't that torque-y either. While it was easily capable of cruising all day at slow speed, it vibrated like crazy at higher speed. One reviewer noted, "When you're overtaking on the highway, you really need to plan out the maneuver."

I'm not sure how well Sooraj planned out its diesel motorcycle strategy, but as this book goes to press, the company is no longer in the motorcycle business (although it still sells a 510cc diesel rickshaw.)

Day 306 – **Royal Enfield Taurus**

Perhaps the only established manufacturer that has offered a diesel motorcycle to the public was Royal Enfield, which sold the Taurus diesel model in India in the '90s.

Enfield probably didn't really want to be in the diesel business, but Sooraj (and other creative Indian mechanics) had been replacing worn-out Bullet motors with small industrial diesels for years. What those conversions lost in performance, they made up in ridiculous fuel mileage. 150 miles per gallon was nothing.

That prompted Royal Enfield to make a deal with Sooraj, which sourced an Italian-designed Lombardini pump motor, manufactured under license in Indian by the Greaves Cotton Company. The Taurus model was sold through Enfield's Indian dealer network until 2002, when it ran afoul of India's new emissions controls. While the Taurus didn't get much love when new it's now a cult bike in India.

Day 307 – **Sommer 462**

The idea of an even-more-agricultural Enfield Bullet appealed to Jochen Sommer, who has taken an oh-so-German approach. Sommer builds 50-60 bikes per year, which are basically blueprinted and improved Bullet chassis, fitted with a 462cc Hatz diesel single.

Sommer's bikes are not particularly cheap, listing for €9,300, nor are they particularly fast; top speeds are only a bit over 60 miles per hour. However, they're rugged and low-maintenance — Sommer fits a belt drive — and they get about 130 miles to the gallon.

The Sommer 462 is one of the best examples of a motorcycle that's so ugly it's cute. For more information: http://www.motorradmanufaktur.de

Day 308 – **Dnepr? Dunno...**

Although Ural is by far the best-known Russian motorcycle in the U.S., there are those who claim that the Dnepr, made in Kiev, Ukraine was the best 'Russian' brand. The factory was founded in 1945, and produced 50-60,000 bikes a year during its Cold War heyday. In 2015, according to the company's annual report, it had fewer than 70 employees, so production numbers are obviously down a bit!

Most Dneprs are sidecar rigs, with a driven sidecar wheel. According to their (Russian-language only) web site, they've experimented with a bunch of weird and wonderful contraptions, including a sidecar-fire truck. But the company is nowhere near as inventive as Dnepr owners, who are… well, imagine if the *Junkyard Wars* was cast at a convention of survivalist preppers.

The result is, there are a few pretty famous YouTube videos of Dnepr sidecar rigs converted to run on Hartz industrial diesel motors.

Day 309 – **Track T-800CDI**

At the other end of the tech spectrum from the Sommer and Dnepr diesel projects, you'll find the Track T-800CDI. Or should I write, "You would have found" in the past tense? The last Track was manufactured by EVA Products Ltd., in the Netherlands, in 2012 — the bike was a victim of the Great Recession, its own high cost, and the low acceptance of the diesel Smart car (it borrowed the same powerplant).

That said, it was nearly a great idea — the brainchild of Erik Vegt, a talented Dutch engineer. Vegt's T-800 was an adventure bike, intended to compete with the likes of the BMW R1200GS. Like the Beemer, the Track had a shaft drive, although it was kept the Smart's CVT transmission, which was pretty unique in a big bike.

The Track had a strong-looking chrome-moly space frame and top-spec components like WP shock and fork, and

Brembo brakes. The diesel motor produced less than 50 horsepower, although it generated a very decent 73 pound-feet of torque. On balance, it was not as fast as a BMW GS, but got terrific fuel mileage.

Vegt sold about 50 of them before giving up on the venture. He wasn't the only guy to see the Smart diesel triple as a potential motorcycle engine though; Neil Laughlin (an engineer in Northern Ireland) and Heiko (a company in Germany) also used that motor in conversions of early 2000s Triumph Tigers.

Day 310 – **Star Twin Thunderstar 1200 TDI**

Maybe it's the legal pot cafés but for whatever reason, the Dutch have a history of very creative but short-lived motorcycle businesses.

One such venture was the Thunderstar 1200 TDI diesel sport bike made by Kees van der Starre — owner of the Star Twin motorcycle shop in the small town of Loenen, about 30 miles east of Amsterdam.

Van der Starre also chose a triple, in this case sourcing a motor normally used in a Volkswagen Lupo compact car. The VW mill was turbocharged, and easily capable of generating more torque than any mass-produced gasoline-powered motorcycle.

The Thunderstar was intended to be a sport bike, right down to its BST carbon wheels. Unfortunately, it was a case of lotsa' smoke, not much fire; only one prototype was ever made.

Day 311 – **Neander 1400 Turbo Diesel**

As you know by now, most diesel motorcycles are Frankenstein's monsters, with motors from one source stitched to a motorcycle chassis from somewhere else. The Neander is more like Frankenstein's own baby — a unique creature that appeared fully formed about 10 years ago, powered by a 1400cc parallel-twin diesel quite unlike any other motor.

Seriously. It has two pistons, but four connecting rods spinning two contra-rotating crankshafts. (You can see an animation of it working at Neander-Motors.com.) The design eliminates the vibration associated with most diesels. The Neander's no cave-man bike; it also features a Bosch common-rail direct-injection system and a turbocharger. The result is 'only' 112 hp at 4,200 rpm, but almost 160 lb-ft of torque.

Coming onto the market just before the recession, with an $85,000 price tag, the Neander 1400 was probably not destined for huge sales numbers. But the company's survived nonetheless, and if you have your heart set on a Neander, you can order one. (The company appears to be shifting its emphasis to outboard motors now.)

Day 312 – **Hero RnT: Less is more, in this case**

A lot of the newer diesels that companies have attempted to bring to market were big, powerful, and expensive. India's Hero motorcycle company has shown a very cool concept bike, the Hero RnT, that's smaller, more modest, and way more versatile.

The RNT is powered by a 150cc single-cylinder diesel motor, which can also double as a generator. And, an electric front-hub motor will give it two-wheel drive capability, too.

Hero claims that when it reaches production, the 150cc diesel will produce nearly 15 horsepower; that's almost certainly optimistic, but even if it can't quite reach the claimed top speed of 45 miles per hour, the RNT could still be a remarkably useful utility vehicle across much of the developing world.

The question is, does Hero really plan to make it? The RnT may have just been a show bike that captured the attention of tech bloggers and left the company stammering that yes, of course, sure they planned to put it into production.

If it ever sees the light of day as a real model, it could be the equivalent of a Honda Cub for the third-world. If that happens, maybe they should call it the Hero 'Runt'.

•

Revisiting England's Mods 'n' Rockers

Britain went into a media frenzy in 1964, when fights erupted between rival youth gangs — the scooter-riding 'Mods' versus motorcycle-riding 'Rockers'.

Day 313 – **The Mods...**

According to Wikipedia, the term 'Mod' derives from 'modernist', and it was first ascribed to a group of hip London jazz fans in the late 1950s. As London entered the "Swinging '60s" the term came to encompass a wider group of clothes-conscious, working class kids in London and the south of England.

The Mods dressed sharply, favoring suits. They rode Vespa and Lambretta scooters, often customized with extra lights and mirrors. They listened to contemporary music, especially soul and R&B from the U.S. and British bands like the The Who, The Yardbirds, and The Small Faces. They danced in music clubs, often under the influence of amphetamines.

Day 314 – **The Rockers…**

As the name implies, the Rockers' musical tastes leaned towards early American rock 'n' roll — Gene Vincent, Eddie Cochran, and Chuck Berry for example. Rockers rode real motorcycles, not scooters, and dressed the part in black leather jackets, jeans, and engineer boots.

Both groups were largely working-class, but the Mods aspired to a more urban (and urbane) image while the Rockers were openly rebellious. By the end of the 1950s, British working class blokes were starting to buy cars like the Morris Minor; as a consequence, motorcycles were relegated to lower-class transport. The last thing the British motorcycle industry needed was bad publicity.

Day 315 – **Doing the Ton**

'The Ton' was slang for 100 miles an hour. Doing the Ton — going 100 or over — was still a bit of an achievement on the bikes of the day. Another name for the Rockers, often used by the sensationalist British press was 'Ton-up Boys'.

In 1964, the J. Arthur Rank chain of movie houses, commissioned a short film called, A Look at Life: Behind the Ton-up Boys. Judging from its breathless optimism, its safe to say the script was approved by the British Motorcycle Industry Association. Still, it's worth searching for it on YouTube.

Day 316 – Café was pronounced 'kaff'

While the Mods were urban, the natural habitat of the Rockers were the 'transport cafés' (what Americans would call truck stops) along British highways. The most famous of them all was the Ace Café, which opened in 1938 on London's North Circular Road.

The Ace Café was bombed flat in WWII, but it was rebuilt after war and experienced its glory days in the 1960s, when Rockers congregated there. At the time, the American rock 'n' roll music they listened to was rarely heard on Britain's state-controlled radio stations, so the Rockers hung out in places like the Ace, with well-stocked juke boxes.

The term 'café racer' referred to both the Rockers themselves, and the motorcycles they modified to ride from one café to the next. (Working class Brits didn't pronounce the accent in 'café'. It was 'kaff'.)

Day 317 – The definitive café racer: Triton

In the early '60s, Nortons were generally thought of as the best-handling bikes. This was down to the patented 'Featherbed' twin-loop frame that was first developed for Norton works racers in 1949. Norton used Featherbed style frames for most of its models in the late '50s, so in the Rockers' heyday, used frames were common.

The definitive café racer of the period was probably a Triton, which was made by putting the best-commonly available motor — a Triumph Bonneville 650 twin — into a Norton frame. There were lots of other 'specials' built on the same principle, including Norbsas (Norton frame/BSA twin) and Norvins (Norton frame, Vincent v-twin.)

Unit-construction Bonnies came out in '63, so in the Mods vs. Rockers period, most Bonnevilles would have been pre-unit construction (with a separate gearbox). Although Norton's twins were not typically as powerful or reliable as Triumphs, a lot of riders preferred the Norton gearbox. So quite a few Tritons mated the Triumph motor to a Norton gearbox.

Day 318 – **The 59 Club**

The definitive Rocker club was, ironically, created in a church. The 59 Club (founded in 1959) got its start as a Church of England youth club in London's poor East End. In 1962, the 59 Club created a Motorcycle Section, which quickly overtook the rest of the club's activities.

Throughout the '60s, the club was run by an Anglican priest, the Reverend Bill Shergold. It was sometimes known as "The Vic's Caff". Membership in 'The 9' grew to the tens of thousands and the club's generally positive image was a counterweight to the otherwise-poor image of Rockers scuffling with Mods.

The club was one of the first places where The Wild One was screened in the UK. (The film had been banned by

UK censors for 15 years — presumably because they feared it would incite biker violence.) The club still exists, and it maintains a web site at www.The59Club.org.uk.

Day 319 – **The Brighton riot**

In the spring of 1964, occasional encounters between groups of Mods and Rockers turned into shoving matches and fights broke out. The first brawl to be widely covered in the British press took place in Clacton, a seaside resort that was a popular destination on holiday weekends. That was over the Easter break.

Over the next long weekend, thousands of Mods rode their scooters south from London, to Brighton (another seaside resort) where they encountered an equally large number of Rockers. A series of running fights ensued, which lasted for a couple of days. The Brighton riots probably ended more because the Mods and Rockers had to get back to work, not because the police finally regained control. Still, the sociologist Stanley Cohen has argued that the Mods vs. Rockers riots were no worse than the fights that routinely broke out at soccer games.

As had happened at Hollister 20 years earlier, newspapers reveled in the story. Both Mods and Rockers became the victims of negative stereotypes by older Britons.

Day 320 – **There's sharp dressing.**
Then there's *sharp dressing*.

If it came to a brawl, the Rockers' motorcycle jackets, boots, and gloves (to say nothing of helmets) were a bit of an advantage. By contrast, the Mods sharp suits were easily ruined and useless as protection.

To even the odds a little, some Mods sewed fishhooks or razor blades under their lapels, so that anyone grabbing them got more than they bargained for.

Day 321 – **Quadrophenia (the album)**

About ten years after the riots, The Who released their second rock opera/concept album, 'Quadrophenia'. The album, which was composed entirely by Pete Townshend, told the story of Jimmy — a scooter-riding Mod — set in London and Brighton. Jimmy has a four-way split personality, hence the album title.

'Tommy' and 'Who's Next' were tough acts to follow for The Who. In 1973 and '74, when the band toured to promote the album, they openly fought on stage at several performances (which you have to admit, suited the subject matter.)

In spite of the band's challenges, Quadrophenia remains one of the better efforts by a rock band to capture teen-aged angst. Townshend later said that the 'Jimmy' character was an amalgamation of several fans he'd met during The Who's early years.

Cool fact: Townshend still rides scooters.

•

Everything old is new again

The French say, "The only things that are new are things that have been forgotten." That's certainly true in motorcycle design. Over the years, there have been any number of engineering 'breakthroughs' that were really just old ideas that'd been rediscovered.

Day 322 – **Monoshock suspension**

Virtually all modern sporting motorcycles, whether designed for on- or off-road use, use a monoshock rear suspension. Those designs pretty much all derive from the Yamaha motocross bike that Hakan Andersson used to win the 1973 250cc World Championship.

That Yamaha 'monocross' design located a long Macpherson strut under the fuel tank. The longer strut allowed Yamaha to build in 50% more suspension travel, and within a year or two there was no point even entering a twin-shock bike in a serious motocross race.

Monoshock designs provided other advantages, even for street bikes that don't need long-travel suspension; notably they're easier to tune and can easily be connected to the frame via linkages that effectively change spring rates throughout the range of suspension travel.

According to Pete Young's excellent Occhio Lungo blog, one of the first motorcycles to locate a single suspension unit under the rider was the Perry Vale, aka the PV.

'Perry Vale' was not the maker's name; the maker was George Elliston. He took the name Perry Vale from the street where his workshop was located. Elliston was awarded a patent for his rear springing system in 1910. PV motorcycles from that time had a triangulated swingarm very similar to the one on that influential '73 Yamaha.

Day 323 – **Belt drive**

Harley-Davidson replaced chain drives with low-maintenance Kevlar belts in the early 1980s. But those were far from the first belt-drive Harleys. All Harleys built before 1912 had belt drives; 1912-'13 models could be ordered with the buyer's choice of a belt or a chain.

Although chains require quite a bit of maintenance, they were a big improvement over those early leather belts, which slipped and didn't last very long at all.

Modern toothed belts were developed for use inside motors, as cam belts. They're strong, lighter than chains, and require essentially no maintenance.

If you're wondering why more sporting motorcycles don't adopt toothed-belt drives, here are two reasons: it's harder to adjust final drive ratios with belt drives, because the length of the belts can't be adjusted, and; most motorcycles 'squat' under hard acceleration. That squat is caused by tension in the drive system, and it can effectively shorten the distance between the countershaft and the rear axle. Chains are better suited to those variable length scenarios.

That's not a problem on most cruisers, because they typically have only a few inches of rear wheel travel.

•

Day 324 – **Rim brakes**

One of the many striking features of Erik Buell's sport bikes are his rim brakes; instead of a caliper grabbing a disc mounted to the front hub, Buell moved the front brake caliper out to wheel rim.

His rationale for doing that was that before your front brake can slow your motorcycle, it first has to overcome the inertia of the spinning wheel itself. You intuitively understand that it's easier to stop the spinning wheel by grabbing the rim than the hub. Mounting the brake rotor to the rim also enabled Buell to design a much lighter front hub and spokes, reducing unsprung weight.

This was pretty much the same rationale used by many motorcycle makers (including BSA) between 1910 and 1920, when 'dummy rim brakes' were fitted to many bikes. These weren't called dummy rim brakes because they were for dummies, they were called that because a second 'dummy' rim was attached to the spokes near the rim. The dummy rim gave the weak, mechanical friction brakes of the day extra leverage, because the forces were applied far from the front hub.

Day 325 – **Hub steering**

Why do almost all modern motorcycles have a telescopic front fork? Good question, because there are lots of reasons *not* to use a conventional fork. For starters, all of the suspension, steering, and braking loads need to be transferred through the same component. A front suspension arrangement with hub-centered steering allows each of those forces to be handled separately.

The Bimota Tesi may be the most famous hub-center-steered motorcycle. The ill-fated Yamaha GTS-1000 was one of the few modern hub-center designs to be mass produced. Neither of those was a commercial success, but the failure of hub-center designs in the market has more to do with the fact that motorcyclists (and motorcycle makers) are surprisingly conservative.

That said, the advantages of hub-centered designs have been apparent for a long time. One notable early example was the 1909 James Safety Model, which featured single-sided hubs at both front and rear — so it was possible to change either tire without even removing the wheels. Price for this 3½ hp model: £48.

Day 326 – **Air intake through the steering head**

The Kawasaki ZX-10R superbike has a trick ram-air intake that channels air around both sides of the steering head and through the frame into the airbox. That probably accounts for a few horsepower at high speed, when it slightly pressurizes the airbox.

Kawasaki wasn't the first motorcycle company to do it, though. The 1980 Can-Am MX-6 motocrosser used exactly the same technique (although the actual intake was located directly behind the number plate, so it's doubtful that it had much of an effect.)

Not-cool fact: Motocross Action magazine rated the MX-6 as one of the ten worst motocross bikes of all time.

Day 327 – **The first 'Slingshot'?**
Maybe it was a Morgan

Henry Frederick Stanley Morgan began producing three-wheeled cars, with two wheels and automotive type steering up front, and a single rear wheel on a motorcycle-type swingarm at the rear around 1910. His design was so effective that versions of it remained in production into the 1950s.

Until WWII, most Morgans were powered by v-twin motorcycle engines, which were mounted in front of the front axle.

Cool fact: Morgan is making three-wheelers again, powered by 121 cu. in. S&S v-twin motors. Less-cool fact: They run around $40 grand.

Day 328 – Cabin motorcycles

The Peraves Monotracer and the Lit C-1 are two ultra-high tech, enclosed 'cabin motorcycles'. Obviously, fully enclosing the rider has potential safety benefits, besides offering improved comfort and weather protection. But the biggest advantage is aerodynamic; a fully enclosed design offers radically improved airflow and can easily double fuel economy at highway speeds.

The advantages of a fully enclosed motorcycle have been known for a long time. For whatever reason, the former Czechoslovakia was a hotbed of creative design of such vehicles, which were called 'dálníks'.

One of the most ingenious dálník designers was Jan Anderlé, who worked in a Czech airplane factory before WWII; he designed and created dálníks in his spare time. If you search for his name and the word dálník on YouTube, you'll find a fascinating bit of film from 1941, which shows Anderlé demonstrating a very well put-together machine.

Not-cool fact: Anderlé escaped to the west after the war, and briefly settled in Belgium. His wife was homesick and convinced him to return to Czechoslovakia which, by then, was under Russian influence. Anderlé was imprisoned for years.

Day 329 – **Vultus? Try Ner-A-Car**

Honda created some buzz (and plenty of head-shaking) when it released the the Vultus NM4 — which puts the rider in a recumbent, feet-forward position. Honda says that 'NM' stands for 'new motorcycle' but the Vultus isn't nearly the first motorcycle with that layout.

One of the most striking early recumbents was the Ner-A-Car. Carl Neracher designed the first one in 1918, and his company produced about 10,000 of them in Syrcacuse, NY between 1921-'27. Most were single-seaters, with 221 cc two-stroke motors.

Although they weren't powerful, they were known for good handling. Erwin 'Cannonball' Baker rode one from New York to Los Angeles, over a little less than a month, in 1922. Neracher also licensed his design for manufacture in the UK, and about 6,500 UK models were made by Sheffield-Simplex in Kingston-on-Thames. Some of the English ones had a 348cc four-stroke motor, and Sturmey-Archer three-speed trannies.

Day 330 – **Worth Knowing: Ernst Henne**

Ernst Henne set over 70 land speed records on BMW motorcycles, in the years prior to WWII. He was also an accomplished road racer, and a skilled off-road rider, competing in several ISDTs in the 1930s.

As a road racer, he was German 750cc champion in 1927. His greatest achievement was winning the '28 Targa Florio race in Sicily. When Germany started building high-speed 'autobahn' highways, BMW often used them for record attempts. Henne set his final record in 1937, exceeding 173 miles per hour in a 500cc BMW streamliner. It stood for 14 years.

Henne was a pilot, although he was rejected by the Luftwaffe, on account of the numerous concussions he'd experienced as a motorcycle racer. Ironically, he lived to be 101!

•

Remember telling your mom you wanted a motorbike?

"You'll kill yourself!" is probably about average, as far as parental reactions go. And do you know *why* they say that? Because motorcycles really *are* that dangerous! As a result, your parents probably encouraged you to take up almost any other sport.

Indeed, athletes from other sports are proof that being young, in top shape, and having great reflexes are no guarantee of safety when it comes to riding motorcycles.

As if you needed yet another warning, here's a list of major leaguers whose careers were interrupted — sometimes permanently — as a result of motorcycle crashes.

Day 331 – **What's the wrist that can happen?**

In March of 2002, the San Francisco Giants were in Scottsdale for spring training. That's where second baseman Jeff Kent decided to practice his wheelies — in spite of the fact that his contract specifically banned motorcycle stunts.

He crashed and broke his wrist, then compounded his problem by getting caught in lie about how it happened. (His story was that he broke his wrist while washing his truck, which was creative though not particularly believable.)

Kent was caught because two witnesses called 911 to report "a guy on a motorcycle was doing wheelies and crashed". He was gone by the time the cops got there, but the Scottsdale PD put two and two together. You might think getting off with a broken wrist was light, but because he was injured in an activity specifically banned in his contract, the Giants docked his pay during the time he was on disabled list. That means his fine for doing wheelies was $33,000 a day.

(The baseball player's association won't let teams bar players from riding motorcycles, but they can ban them from stunting.)

Day 332 – Big Ben rings his bell

In 2005, Ben Roethlisberger became the youngest quarterback to lead his team (the Pittsburgh Steelers) to a Super Bowl championship. A year later his career nearly came to an end when he crashed his Suzuki Hayabusa while riding without a helmet.

Steelers coach Bill Cowher had warned 'Big Ben' about the dangers of motorcycle riding a year earlier, after the Cleveland Browns' tight end Kellen Winslow Jr. tore knee ligaments in a crash that put him out for an entire season. Steelers legend Terry Bradshaw had also told Roethlisberger to wait until he retired to ride motorcycles.

Roethlisberger's mother was killed in a car crash when he was a little kid. And, for a guy whose job involves wearing a helmet, it's ironic he chose to ride without one. (Pennsylvania had a mandatory helmet law from the late '60s until 2003, when it was amended.)

I suppose that a helmet would've been too much to ask, since Roethlisberger didn't even have a motorcycle license. Luckily, he absorbed the impact with his face, not his skull.

Day 333 – **Unlucky Luc**

Luc Bourdon was a promising 21 year-old NHL rookie, who went back home to New Brunswick for the summer break in 2008. He got a motorcycle license, and two weeks later he bought a brand-new GSX-R1000. What could possibly go wrong, eh?

His girlfriend and his mom both tried to talk him out of it. His girlfriend was actually following him in her car when he ran wide on a curve and body-checked an oncoming semi.

Day 334 – **Destinee Blue**

You don't have to be male, a major leaguer, or even at the controls to end your athletic career in a motorcycle crash. Destinee Blue was a standout high school and college basketball player in Wisconsin, who played pro women's ball in Europe before returning to Milwaukee to recuperate from a knee injury.

Blue, who was 25 in 2014, was on the back of a 40-year-old friend's bike. He was weaving in and out of traffic at a reported 75 miles per hour when a car turned left in front of them. They hit the car hard enough to spin it around 180°. The rider was wearing a helmet but it didn't protect him; another helmet was found at the scene, but it was not on Destinee Blue's head. Both rider and passenger were dead at the scene.

You might think this is evidence that women can be as stupid as men. But sadly, it seems the most common way they're stupid is, they make stupid choices in boyfriends.

Day 335 – **Knock yourself out**

Diego 'Chico' Corrales held the WBC, WBO, and Ring Magazine lightweight titles. In 2005, the Boxing Writers Association rated one of his title fight against José Luis Castillo as 'fight of the year'.

Two years to the day after the best fight of his career, Chico was riding his brand-new Gixxer 1000 when he attempted to pass another vehicle at high speed. It's impossible to know if he was simply trying to pass it, or was actually trying to pass though it — either way, he hit it so hard and with so much closing speed that he flew 100 feet through the air, landing in an oncoming traffic lane, where he was hit again.

One imagines his arrival at the pearly gates of heaven. "But ref," Chico might say to St. Peter, "He hit me while I was down."

Corrales' blood alcohol content was 0.25 — triple the legal limit.

Day 336 – Quoth the raven, 'Nevermore'.

If there's one 'peak danger' moment for pro athletes, it's the off-season after their rookie pro year.

Tray Walker was always an underdog. He grew up in the Liberty City neighborhood of Miami (where the median household income is about half the U.S. average) and played for Texas Southern — a college that didn't typically get much love from NFL scouts. He was picked in the fourth round of the 2015 draft, and played in eight games in his rookie year as a Baltimore Raven.

Baltimore has a big outlaw dirt bike scene, and that may be what influenced Walker to take up riding an unlicensed dirt bike when, after his rookie season, he returned to Liberty City.

Typically, when athletes mess themselves up on motorcycles, they're at fault. That was perhaps not Walker's case; he was not under the influence of drugs or booze, and doesn't appear to have been speeding. He was hit in an intersection by a vehicle that should have stopped. Walker was, however, not wearing a crash helmet. Florida repealed its mandatory helmet law in 2000. Helmet use fell from nearly 100% to around 50% of all motorcyclists over the next decade.

Day 337 – Turning a life into a cautionary tale

Jason David "Jay" Williams was one of the top college basketball players of his generation, drafted second overall

by the Chicago Bulls in 2002. He was another pro afflicted
by that never-gonna'-make-to-sophomore jinx. During the
off season, he was riding his Yamaha R6 in Chicago —
without a crash helmet, or for that matter, a license —
when a wheelie went wrong and he smashed the left side
of his body into a light pole.

Pretty much every ligament in his left knee was torn, but
the worst aspect of the injury was nerve damage. To add
insult to injury, his Bulls contract explicitly forbade riding
motorcycles, so the team could have placed him on
waivers without paying him a salary. (The team gave him
$3 million to cover the cost of his rehabilitation.)

Williams never played professionally again, but he did
eventually put his life back together. He's worked as an
agent and broadcaster, and recently wrote a book, *"Life Is
Not an Accident: A Memoir of Reinvention"*.

•

Day 338 – **Weirdly compelling motorcycle movie:** *Quadrophenia*

The Mods vs. Rockers riots happened in the mid- '60s. It
was the early '70s before The Who produced their
'Quadrophenia' concept album set in that period. By the
time this film was made in 1979, the real Mods and
Rockers were middle-aged.

That said, it does a good job of taking us back to the
famous Brighton riot.

As one British reviewer notes on 'IMDb', *"A young man
joins the British mod movement and gains a feeling of*

belonging and importance, but this makes him even more disenfranchised from his boring 9 to 5 life. Britain's answer to 'Rebel Without A Cause'...has far too much going for it to be ignored. Especially if you are working class and come from the UK."

•

Day 339 – **Worth Knowing: T.E. Lawrence**

Thomas Edward Lawrence (aka 'Lawrence of Arabia') was an avid motorcyclist who is said to have owned no less than eight different Brough Superior motorcycles – one of which is on display at the Imperial War Museum in London.

Lawrence was killed in a motorcycle accident, near his home in Dorset (southern England) in 1935. He was 46 years old. It's said that a dip in the road concealed two kids on bicycles from his view, and that he crashed after swerving to avoid them.

He survived in a coma for five days, during which time he was attended by a famous British neurosurgeon (Dr. Hugh Cairns) who then embarked on a study motorcycle riders' head injuries. Cairns' research helped to encourage the development and use of the modern crash helmet.

•

Day 340 – **The famous motorcycle hardly anyone's seen**

There are iconic motorcycle photos that everyone — whether they like motorcycles or not — have seen. For example, picture Rollie Free wearing nothing but a bathing suit, setting a land speed record on the Bonneville Salt

Flats. That's an image we all have buried in our subconscious.

But there's an even more famous motorcycle picture, of 'Wild Bill' Gelbke, astride the home-made motorcycle he called 'Roadog'. Gelbke's bike was seventeen feet long and weighed over 3,000 pounds. In the photo, he's stopped in front of a roadhouse in eastern Wisconsin. Gelbke is wearing leather boots and trousers, a sawn-off denim vest and pair of heavy gloves, and a peaked cap.

The photo was shot in 1970 by Ralph Goldsmith. He was the publisher, editor, and sole reporter for the Bascobel Dial newspaper in Bascobel, WI. If there was an award for the image most reproduced without any payment or copyright acknowledgment, Goldsmith would win it.

His black-and-white photo, which originally ran in the Dial, has been blown up, copied and reproduced countless times. Unauthorized posters appear on the walls of bars and roadhouses that Gelbke himself may have visited across the upper Midwest. And yet he photographer never earned a cent for the photo.

Day 341 – **Why did they call him 'Wild Bill'?**

William Gelbke was born in Green Bay, WI in 1938. He studied engineering at the University of Southern California and worked in the aerospace industry, before returning to the Chicago area. In the early 1960s, he opened up a motorcycle shop on Cicero Avenue.

Gelbke set out to build a motorcycle to his own specifications — he wanted an effortless 100 mph cruising speed, long range, and reliability. In general, he felt that automotive components were superior to motorcycle components, which led him to create a motorcycle about the size of a car.

Other people were intimidated by the sheer size of the motorcycles he created, but Gelbke was even stronger than his stocky frame suggested. He had a reputation as a fearsome brawler.

Day 342 – **Roadog I & II**

Gelbke built the first Roadog in 1965. He chose the 153 cu. in., inline four-cylinder motor from a Chevy II car with a Powerglide two-speed automatic transmission. He created a spectacular trailing-link front fork with four shock absorbers; the handlebars alone were longer than many motorcycles.

Roadog was 17 feet long, and weighed a reported 3,280 pounds. If the thought of getting that beast on and off the kickstand scares you, don't worry; it doesn't have a kickstand. When it came time to leave it, Gelbke lowered four hydraulic rams that kept it level.

Although Roadog seems patently ridiculous, Gelbke rode it, a lot. It was sort of a mechanical Loch Ness monster, appearing for a moment on the roads of the upper Midwest, leaving people rubbing their eyes and wondering if they were seeing things. According to legend, Gelbke thought nothing of hopping on Roadog and riding from his home in Wisconsin to Oklahoma because he thought the steaks were better there; he'd ride to Texas for a beer.

Gelbke built a second Roadog, very similar to the first, for one of his friends.

John Burns, then writing for 'Motorcyclist' magazine, test rode Roadog in 1995. He crashed it, luckily at walking speed. The result was one of the funniest stories the magazine ever ran.

Day 343 – Gelbke Grasshopper & Bulldog

Roadog was not Gelbke's only attempt to create a uniquely massive and powerful motorcycle. He built at least two motorcycles using a six-cylinder 'boxer' motor from a Chevrolet Corvair mated to a VW transmission. The rear tire on that bike was originally sold for use as a front tire on a farm tractor. That tire was called a 'Grasshopper', which is apparently why Gelbke gave that name to one of those bikes.

Although it weighs at least a thousand pounds and has its own custom made plunger rear suspension, Gelbke used a conventional front fork on the Grasshopper, sourced from a Harley-Davidson Hydra-Glide.

It's a weird testament to Gelbke that virtually every motorcycle he ever made has been preserved. The Grasshopper was restored by a guy in Green Bay. He describes it as "low and well-balanced" but the clutch pull is a bitch. He built another, similar one that he called the 'Bulldog'.

Day 344 – Gelbke Auto-Four

The closest Gelbke ever got to his dream of mass-producing a heavyweight cruiser with automotive range, comfort, and reliability was the Gelbke Auto-Four. A total of seven or eight Auto-Fours were built, and Gelbke rode one of them from Chicago to California in 1972, where it was tested for Cycle News.

The Auto-Four had a four cylinder British Leyland car motor, with a four-speed tranny. It had a reverse gear and a parking brake; two niceties that were useful on a bike that, depending on accessories and configuration, was reported as weighing from 950 to 1,300 pounds. (I'm more inclined to believe the latter figure!) The Auto-Four's wheelbase was about twenty inches longer than an Indian Chief's.

Some Auto-Fours were supplied with Hydra-Glide front forks, others were sold with Gelbke's own leading-link front fork.

Day 345 – **He fought the law, and the law won**

By 1978, Gelbke had given up on his dream of becoming a motorcycle manufacturer. He'd closed his shop in Chicago and returned to Green Bay. He was 43 years old.

There are a number of stories circulating about why, exactly, Wild Bill ran afoul of the Green Bay police. I've read that he was involved in a domestic dispute, or that there was a dispute involving a dog. Craig Constantine, a TV producer who made a documentary about Gelbke says that Bill had purchased a semi, and that the cops thought he was moving dope as well as truckloads of vegetables.

Whatever their motivation, about a dozen Green Bay cops arrived at Gelbke's house, on the outskirts of Green Bay, one Sunday morning in November. According to one account, Gelbke had stolen one cop's girlfriend decades earlier when they went to high school together.

They called for him to throw his gun out. He may have fired his gun (that fact's in dispute, along with all the others) but the incident ended with Gelbke shot and killed.

Day 346 – Unlike their creator, Roadog I and II survived

Roadog I was acquired by a guy named Anthony Shablak, who eventually sold it to Steve 'Doc' Hopkins. The bike was displayed in his Doc's Harley-Davidson of Shawano County dealership, but it's since been sold to a private collector.

Roadog II was acquired by Buzz Walneck, of Walneck's Cycle Trader fame. Buzz trailered the behemoth around for years, using it to develop publicity for his magazine. He sold it to a collector, who has since loaned it to the National Motorcycle Museum in Anamosa, Iowa.

The National Motorcycle Museum's worth a detour if you're ever passing through the upper Midwest.

•

"Over there!" A selective history of motorcycles in the U.S. Army

The first time American motorcycles were used in combat was in about 1916, when John "Black Jack" Pershing routed Pancho Villa's forces in the Mexican border regions. As the story goes, William S. Harley personally supervised the creation of Harley-Davidson sidecar rigs, equipped with machine guns.

Who hasn't wanted a machine-gun mount on his motorcycle from time to time? I'll tell you what, if more of us carried that kind of heat while riding, we'd soon stop hearing car drivers' say, "I just didn't see him, officer."

Day 347 – **The first motorcycles roll under Black Jack Pershing**

Pershing was called 'Black Jack' because he once commanded a battalion of African-American 'Buffalo Soldiers' during the Indian Wars. But his career extended to commanding all U.S. forces in Europe in the First World War—from chasing renegade Indians on horseback to fighting Germans with tanks and aircraft.

Part of the increasingly mechanized way of warfare was, of course, the use of more motorcycles. The U.S. Army bought 80,000 motorcycles for that war, including 20,000 Harley-Davidsons and 50,000 Indians (the kind made in Springfield, MA not the kind Black Jack rounded up in Montana early in his career!)

Day 348 – **Harley interprets a War Department request loosely**

In 1938, the War Department put out a request for a new motorcycle. The specifications were that it displace 500cc, be capable of sustained slow-speed use without overheating, be relatively waterproof to enable a stream crossing, and be able to cruise at 65 miles per hour.

Indian took the War Department's request as gospel, and produced its Model 641, based on the civilian Junior Scout. Indian reduced the compression ratio in that motor, in the anticipation of uneven fuel quality. There were a few other changes, too: the front fork was lengthened for increased ground clearance, mudguards were lifted to prevent mud from gathering between fenders and tires, and a better air filter was fitted.

William Harley, however, was sure that the military needed a 750cc motorcycle. (Perhaps not coincidentally because Harley had the proven W-series motor ready to go.)

Harley proved to be right. In fact, the War Department came back to Indian and told them the Model 641 was fine in every respect except that it was too slow. Indian then offered the Model 741, based on the 45 cu.in. Sport Scout.

Day 349 – "The Russians' (parts) are coming!"

During WWII, the Harley-Davidson WLA served in the American forces, while the slightly different WLC model was deployed with Canadians. The bikes had 45 cu.in. flathead motors that were already about a decade out of date. The U.S. Army acquired about 90,000 WLAs, and many thousands were also sent to the Soviet Union as part of the 'lend-lease' program. To this day, when American collectors and restorers need WLA parts, they find them in the former Soviet Union.

Every U.S. armored division included 540 motorcycles (either H-D WLAs or Model 741 Indians) in its Table of Organization and Materiel. Almost all of those bikes saw dispatch or military police-type service. American forces rarely used motorcycles for troop transport or combat purposes any more, so they weren't commonly equipped with sidecars, as seen on the German side.

Day 350 – Jeep zaps our Zundapp

American forces were impressed with captured German motorcycles. Several specimens were shipped back to the U.S., and Harley-Davidson hurriedly developed its own boxer-twin military bike. About 1,000 of those XA models were built for evaluation.

The XA is usually described as a copy of the BMW R71, although the Wehrmacht's best motorcycle was the Zundapp KS750, which was always delivered in sidecar configuration. It had a driven sidecar wheel and a locking differential, and was unstoppable if not particularly agile.

The Harley-Davidson XA may well have seen service but for one thing: by the time it was ready, the Jeep was ubiquitous. The Jeep weighed just 1,275 pounds and could be supplied for less than $750. As it was, the WLA model continued to see service all through the Korean War.

Day 351 – Indian gets the shaft, too

While the XA is the most famous of the WWII prototypes, Indian also built a shaft-drive sidecar hack for the army's evaluation.

Indian built their shaft-drive bike by turning a Scout motor 90 degrees in the frame, and slightly widening the v-angle. The result looked a lot like a Moto Guzzi. The Wigwam produced about a thousand of them, and designated it the Model 841.

In 1944, the War Department abruptly canceled motorcycle contracts, leaving Indian with a lot of unsold inventory. The reason was, U.S. had enough motorcycles in the European theater, and commanders saw little use for them in the war in the Pacific.

Indian stripped the military equipment off the unsold 741s and sold them to the public at a discount, along with some 841s. War surplus motorcycles are often credited with kick-starting American 'chopper' culture, just as returning veterans are, um, 'credited' with starting the first outlaw motorcycle gangs.

Day 352 – **Q: When will a minibike go 100 mph?
A: When its 'chute won't open.**

The British loved their 'special operations' commandos. One of the Special Operations Executive's projects was a tiny motorcycle, designed for airborne operations. The idea was that 'Welbikes' would give paratroopers improved mobility after deployment.

Welbikes were made by Excelsior Motor Company, in Birmingham (England). They were powered by a 98cc two-stroke motor, which gave the machine a top speed of about 30 miles an hour. It could go about 90 miles on its 1-gallon tank of fuel.

The 71-pound(!) machine was designed to collapse into a standard parachute airdrop container, which was a cylinder about 51" long and just 15" across!

Not to be outdone, U.S. Airborne troops were also issued motorbikes. In the U.S. case, they adapted Powell Streamliner scooters, made in Compton, CA. They had 2½ hp engines, and a claimed top speed of 40 mph. Civilian versions retailed for $129, in 1941 (About $2,100 today.)

Very few Welbikes were successfully used as intended. Nor do I know of any Powell Streamliners that were air-dropped. However, both vehicles were popular as runabouts on air bases.

After the war, Brockhouse Engineering took over the Welbike and sold it as the Corgi. It was also exported to the U.S. and sold as the Indian 'Papoose'.

Interesting fact: Powell went on to produce some very innovative pickup trucks, usually on Plymouth chassis. Those are now highly sought-after collectibles.

Day 353 – **Nam's Angels**

Motorcycles were rarely used in Vietnam War combat operations. One exception was the Reconnaissance Patrol of the 3d Battalion, 22d Infantry, nicknamed 'Nam's Angels'.

The patrol was led by four motorcyclists under the command of Lieutenant Colonel Robert Carmichael, who wanted a quick means of moving soldiers around the maze of small trails in War Zone C, a marshy area near the Cambodian border.

The one photo I've ever found of the team shows them on what appear to be stock Honda CB175s! Although this group was not well documented, it's known to have been effective. They could travel quickly enough to catch the enemy in the act of setting up mortar and rocket sites. You might think that the Nam's Angels would be laughed off, on their CB175, but they were backed up by a Jeep equipped with a belt-fed machine gun.

Day 354 – **Harley acquires Armstrong in the '80s**

In the 1980s, there was an obscure British manufacturer called Armstrong, which made a trail bike powered by a 500cc Rotax single. Armstrong's MT500 military motorcycle was battle-tested in the Falklands.

In the 1980s, the U.S. military put out a call for new motorcycles. Obviously, they favored an 'American' bike. Rather than develop a machine from scratch (or reconfigure some Aermacchi design) Harley-Davidson simply bought Armstrong.

The U.S., Canadian, and Jordanian armed forces used MT500s. A few smaller MT350E versions—the 'E' indicates electric start—were also deployed.

Day 355 – **Diesel has its day in the '90s**

The MT500 was often supplanted by the M1030, which was basically a mil-spec Kawasaki KLR250. The little Kawi had a lot to recommend it. It was cheap, light, user-friendly, and tougher than it looked. If a more powerful bike was needed, they called in its big brother; the M1030B1 was a mil-spec KLR650.

Those were good options, but recent Middle-Eastern wars —both of which underlined the logistical challenge of fighting far from your own territory—convinced the military that if it was going to use motorcycles, they should run on the same fuel used by the rest of its trucks and armor. The call went out to supply motorcycles that would run on diesel.

Hayes Diversified Technologies then supplied a few M1030M1 motorcycles, which are basically a KLR650 rolling chassis, with a 611cc, 30hp motor. Thanks to

Hayes' ingenuity, the M1030M1 is capable of running on almost anything, including JP8 aviation fuel. It gets almost 100 miles per gallon (diesel) at 55 miles per hour, giving it a 400-mile range.

The idea of a bike that out-KLRed a KLR generated a lot of buzz amongst civilian adventure riders. They were bummed that no civilian version was ever offered. As this book goes to press, Hayes describes itself as an R&D company only. The implication is that it's not even supplying the U.S. military any more.

Day 356 – **Special bikes for Spec Ops**

Those Nam's Angels realized that motorcycles enabled them to move fast and hit the enemy at unexpected times and places. Coalition forces in Afghanistan learned that too, the hard way, when Taliban guerillas used motorcycles to conduct quick raids, then move out of range before U.S. and allied forces had a chance to respond.

Before long, U.S. Spec Ops were pressing dirt bikes into service. Two uniquely American motorcycles have now been adapted for their use.

The Christini AWD (gasoline powered) motorcycle enables soldiers who are not expert off-road riders to handle tough terrain. And Zero has made a special, blacked-out version of its nearly silent electric dirt bike—a model called the MMX. It's not only quiet, but it has a lower heat signature than almost any other vehicle, and can ford rivers at a depth of up to three feet.

Day 357 – **Crocker motorcycles, *et al***

Considering the legendary status of the Crocker
Motorcycle Company, it's surprising how few motorcycles
Al Crocker actually manufactured. All told, there were as
few as 200 original Crockers, and for years the brand was
not particularly sought-after by collectors. But the
performance and quality of Crocker's twins is now
appreciated and fans of the marque believe they were the
best American motorcycles made between the World Wars.

Crockers are now among the most valuable American
motorcycles. In 2015, a '42 'Big Tank' twin sold for nearly
$400,000. So, who was Al Crocker and what was it about
those motorcycles that, today, makes them so sought-after?

Day 358 – A Northwestern alum heads west...

Crocker was born in 1882. He was trained as an engineer
at Northwestern, in Illinois. After graduating, he went to
work at the Aurora Automatic Machinery Co., in Aurora
IL. That was the company that made Thor motors and
motorcycles.

Thor also provided castings to George Hendee's Indian
bicycle company. When Indian started making
'motocycles', Hendee and Oscar Hedstrom sent their
prototypes to Aurora, so that company could provide the
needed castings for mass production.

Al Crocker struck up a friendship with the Indian
founders. Those were the days of board-track racing; after
Indian star Eddy Hasha was killed, Crocker fell in love
with Gertrude, his young widow. Crocker ran an Indian
dealership in Denver; he was both a dealer and Midwest
distributor in Kansas City in the 1920s, before moving to

Los Angeles, where he purchased an existing Indian dealership.

Day 359 – Build a better ~~mousetrap~~ motorcycle, Part I: The singles

In Los Angeles, Crocker and his shop's chief mechanic Paul Bigsby made their own OHV heads for Indian 101 Scout motorcycles. They sold quite a few conversion kits that greatly improved the performance of the popular Scout.

By the early 1930s, the board tracks had given way to safer racing on dirt ovals. On the west coast, nighttime speedway races became popular entertainment. Crocker's first complete motorcycles were 500cc single-cylinder speedway racers, which appeared in 1933.

Over the next few years, Crocker sold 40-50 of his single-cylinder production racers.

Day 360 – Better ~~mousetrap~~ motorcycle, Part II: The twins

In 1936, as America dug itself out of the Great Depression, Crocker began offering an OHV twin that was notably faster than anything Harley-Davidson or Indian had to offer. His first twins were 61 cu. in. 45° v-twins that boasted 'hemi' heads.

That first Crocker model weighed 475 pounds and generated 55-60 horsepower at 5,800 rpm. One of the secrets to that impressive power output was that Crocker and Bigsby were among the first guys to realize that bigger wasn't always better when it came to intake manifolds; by restricting intake size, they optimized turbulence for a better fuel-air mix.

Day 361 – Hemi, or parallel-valve?
Small Tank, or Big Tank?

The first 17 Crocker twins were hemis, but that design had valve-train that was prone to wear. So Crocker designed a 'parallel-valve' head.

The parallel-valve head was not that much of a compromise, performance-wise. In 1940, Sam Parriott rode a measured mile at almost 137 miles per hour on Muroc Dry Lake.

Most Crocker twins are characterized as either 'Small Tank' or 'Big Tank' models. The first ones were sold with a cast-aluminum 2½-gallon fuel tank. Later on — beginning in '39 — they were sold with tanks that held three gallons. Those ones were called 'Big Tank' models and, after the fact, people started calling the earlier models 'Small Tank' Crockers.

Day 362 – America's 'Brough Superior'

Like that famous British manufacturer, every Crocker was pretty much tailor-made. Buyers could specify displacements up to 91 cu. in. and compression ratios from 7:1 up to 11:1. They were free to choose colors (even of the frame) and controls, coil or magneto ignition, and could specify different wheelbases.

Even the base models were capable of hitting 110 miles an hour; according to legend, Crocker offered a refund to any customer who was beaten in a race by a stock Indian or Harley — but he never had to make good on it.

Despite the twins' impressive performance, Crocker may have sold as few as 125 of them from 1936-'42. According to motorcycle historian Harry V. Sucher, Crocker cast all his aluminum parts in-house, and the bikes were prone to leaking oil. They also had a reputation for being hard to start. But Crocker's real problem was that as a small manufacturer, he had to charge about $100 more than Harley-Davidson or Indian. That was a big surcharge in the days when a new EL model Harley was $380.

Day 363 – Better ~~mousetrap~~ motorcycle, Part III: The scooters

After the U.S. entered the war, Crocker was unable to get the materials (notably the large quantity of aluminum) required to produce the twins. But, there was a need for cheap, efficient transportation in American cities.

Floyd Clymer convinced Crocker to design a scooter, and the result was the Crocker Scootabout. It had a brought-in 2.3 horsepower air-cooled motor. In magazine ads, Clymer claimed it got 100 miles to the gallon, and was capable of 35 miles per hour.

Crocker designed it with car-like accelerator and brake pedals. It had a raked-out front fork that was advertised as 'co-pilot steering' — meaning, the rider could control it with his or her knees!

At the time, there were several rival scooter manufacturers in the Los Angeles area. Only about 50 Scootabouts were made.

Day 364 – Better ~~mousetrap~~ ~~motorcycle~~ guitar.
Wait a minute. 'Guitar'?

One of the secrets of Crocker's success was the ingenuity of his chief mechanic and die-maker, Paul A. Bigsby. But Bigsby's actually famous for something altogether different: The Bigsby Vibrato. You may not have heard of it, but you've certainly *heard* it, because it's that lever on an electric guitar that allows the guitarist to bend notes.

The Bigsby Vibrato came about when Merle Travis, a popular western musician who was also a motorcyclist asked him if he could fix the worn out Kaufman vibrato on his Gibson guitar. Bigsby went a step further and created his own improved mechanism from scratch.

After WWII, the mechanic shifted his emphasis entirely to guitars. Although Les Paul is typically credited with making the first electric guitar, it was really just a pine slab. Paul Bigsby was the first person to make what we now know as a solid-body guitar. (Les Paul, Leo Fender, and Bigsby were all pals who freely shared their ideas.)

There's still a Bigsby company, making vibratos and high-end electric guitars. The guitars that Bigsby himself crafted are, like Crocker motorcycles, highly sought-after by collectors and have sold for up to $80,000.

Day 365 – **Most under-rated U.S. state for motorcycle riding: Arkansas**

My friends who live in the Midwest will probably be mad at me for making this the last entry in this book. (Not because they think it should have come up earlier, but rather because they wish I'd left it out.)

Arkansas is the best-kept motorcycling secret in America. Smooth roads twist through the Ozarks, drawing sport bike riders to the locally famous 'Pig Trail' – a road that rivals North Carolina's better-known 'Tail of the Dragon' in terms of the quality of ride, without the squids and over-policing!

Cruiser riders flock to Fayetteville every September for Bikes, Blues, and BBQ – a festival billed as "the largest charitable gathering of motorcycles in the U.S.

And dual-sport riders aren't left out either. It's probably no accident that the famous Trans-America Trail passes through Arkansas.

One of the best ways to get an overall introduction to the state's trails and tracks is to register for the three-day Arkansas 500 dual-sport ride, held each spring.

So next time you're planning a motorcycle vacation, consider Arkansas. You won't be disappointed. I can't say as much for my friends, who'll be disappointed that I've let their secret out.

Also available in limited quantities directly from
www.bikewriter.com...

One Man's Island
One of my friends, the Canadian film-maker Peter
Riddihough, spent a good part of 2002 shadowing me on
the Isle of Man. His documentary film, *One Man's Island*,
is an insider's look at my preparation for the TT, and the
races themselves. Selection: Calgary International Film
Festival, Montreal World Film Festival.
DVD, 2 hours, Standard Definition.
$24.95
Please note: Shipped to Canada and the U.S. only.

BMW Racing Motorcycles: The Mastery of Speed
A history of BMW's racing efforts, chronicled by Laurel
Allen and Mark Gardiner, from the formation of the
company after the First World War, until the early 2000s.
Hundreds of great photos from BMW's private archives.
Hardcover, 175 pages
$34.95
Please note: Shipped to U.S. only. Sorry! The United
States Postal Service no longer offers international surface
mail. As a result, it costs me more than the book's worth to
mail it beyond the U.S.

Made in the USA
Charleston, SC
14 November 2016